With over 30 stellar years in the food industry behind him and a plethora of awards to his name, Matt Moran is the tour de force behind some of Australia's most celebrated dining establishments: Aria, Chiswick and North Bondi Fish, to name just a few. It's safe to say he is an Australian food icon.

At the heart of every one of his endeavours lies a passion for fresh, seasonal produce and simplicity in ingredients.

Matt is a frequent contributor to food publications globally and he has been a presenter, judge and host on many much-loved Australian and international TV shows, most recently on the top-rating *Great Australian Bake-off*. This is his fifth cookbook.

For more, visit **mattmoran.com.au**

Matt Moran's
Australian Food

Matt Moran's
Australian Food
COAST + COUNTRY

MURDOCH BOOKS
SYDNEY · LONDON

INTRODUCTION

Sometimes I have to pinch myself. To think of where I started and where I am now – it wasn't necessarily a logical progression, and I have my career in food to thank for it. I consider myself so lucky to have discovered cooking when and where I did, as I've been able to witness and be a part of the evolution of Australian food into what it is today: world class, ever-changing and, quite simply, inspiring.

My early childhood years were spent on a dairy farm, but we moved to Sydney's western suburbs when I was nine. Dad still had a small farm at Taralga we'd visit most weekends and it was there I developed an interest in butchery that remains today. Apart from my weekend life on the farm, my suburban life was little different to that of my peers.

I'd love to say I was bitten by the cooking bug at the age of five and always knew it was what I wanted to do, but the truth is I came to cooking by chance, really. It was my way out of school, which wasn't my favourite thing, and after an inauspicious start at Parramatta RSL, I began an apprenticeship in 1985 at La Belle Helene in Roseville, on Sydney's Upper North Shore. In retrospect, the day I got that job was the day that changed my life forever. Working in that kitchen opened my eyes to the possibilities of food and I was hooked. Over 30 years later, I still am. I may have fallen into it, but cooking remains a deep and abiding passion, not least for its ability to connect people. I love that Australians in general have fallen in love with cooking too – these days we're a food-obsessed country.

As part of that national obsession, I'm often asked to define Australian food. What is it exactly? It's something I've asked myself many times during the writing of this book.

As a relatively young nation, it's fair to say that Australian food isn't tied to tradition in quite the same way that many other cuisines are; there's no single dish that sums us up, nor is there a singular style of cooking that can be called quintessentially Australian. As a country, we're always changing, and the same goes for Australian food. Our population continues to transform with the influx of different migrant groups, all bringing elements of their food culture to our shores, layering it upon what's already here and threading complexity and diversity into the way we eat and cook.

Aussie food truly reflects the multicultural nature of our society and we're all the better for it. No longer do we eat meat and three veg every day, which was the way I grew up. We're just as likely to have sushi for lunch as we are to have a Vegemite sandwich; more likely to tuck into an excellent curry for dinner as have the grilled sausages and chops that were such a part of my childhood.

We like to call ourselves the lucky country, and when it comes to local produce, these words couldn't be more true. It's almost become clichéd in Australia to say so, but our food has become hugely produce-centred. From the fanciest city restaurants to the most remote outback pub or your neighbour's kitchen, this is a shift that's happened within a generation. Think about this concept for a minute. How many other world cuisines can truly claim such a focus on produce? A handful only.

Our varied climates support diverse crops within the one country, and in our home kitchens we've been trying out this new produce, loving it and expecting and getting more from our farmers. When I started cooking in commercial kitchens 30 years ago, there was one variety of tomato – maybe two. Now, there are any number of heirloom varieties, and a simple tomato salad is a far more exciting dish.

The same goes for our other fruit and vegetables, our dairy products and even our pulses and grains. There's now so much great produce available, so much variety. No longer does lettuce equal iceberg only – we all have access to at least a dozen different kinds of salad greens. Some of this broadening is because of our cultural diversity, while some is due to a more widely travelled population – people saw what was available overseas and questioned why it wasn't available here. As consumers, we have more power than we realise and have the ability to drive what is available.

Aussie produce continues to go from strength to strength. We produce Wagyu beef that's so great we export it to the very discerning Japanese market, while our relatively new truffle industry has been so successful we sell truffles back to the French. No longer is pork dry and flavourless, as it was back when I started out – instead there's a focus on rare breeds reared for flavour and succulence.

Our natural resources are amazing too – our vast coastline means we have access to some of the best seafood in the world, not to mention the fact that with a range of water temperatures, we're able to enjoy cold-water fish such as salmon, ocean trout and King George whiting, as well as tropical reef fish – think coral trout, red emperor and our famous barramundi. The variety is mind-boggling and it's hard to believe that back in the day (and that's only a couple of decades ago), most seafood and fish was sold frozen. Compare that to our fish markets, which boast the freshest of fish, crustaceans and shellfish, and it's easy to see that we've come a long way.

We're also becoming increasingly interested in provenance – the whys and hows of food production. We're asking where our food comes from, how it's been reared and whether it has been ethically produced. These are all important questions, which push producers to do better.

All of this contributes towards making Australian food into what I believe is some of the best in the world. It's a big call, I know, but I unashamedly stake that claim. We are now the envy of the world and a food-lover's destination. We should be proud of how far we've come, and continue to expand our cooking horizons.

Ultimately, the definition of Australian food is very personal. Someone who lives in rural Australia will have a different definition to a coastal city-dweller. As an eighth-generation Australian, my definition is likely to be different to that of someone who has a parent or grandparent from another country.

My take on Australian food is deeply influenced by my upbringing, my career path, by travelling and by the amazing produce I am lucky enough to come across every day in my restaurant kitchens. It's the blending of these different experiences that forms the heart of my cooking, and I believe it's also indicative of the way Australian food in general has evolved. We're making our own traditions, taking bits and pieces of all the cultural influences that are at play, putting our spin on them – it's exciting stuff.

This book is divided into two sections, which very much reflect the dual aspects of my life: the coast and the country. I live in Sydney, close to the coast, but I also continue the connection to the land that began in my childhood. Today, Dad and I have a 2000-acre property, about three hours drive west of Sydney, just beyond the Blue Mountains. We have dairy cows, fat lambs and pigs, and have just put in our first truffles. I'm proud to be able to say I'm a fourth-generation farmer.

My life – and the way I cook – is greatly influenced by these two very different locations, so it made sense to me to split this book along these lines. The way I cook when I'm at home in Sydney is different to how and what I cook when I'm at the farm, but the common element is that the dishes you'll find in this book are very much about home-cooking. Although I'm inspired and excited by what's happening in my restaurant kitchens, at home I'll strip it back and simplify, and let the produce lead. The recipes you'll find in this book are just some of the things I love to cook for family and for friends. They're approachable, but in the mix you'll also find dishes that are perfect for special occasions and celebrations. This is the Australian food I love, and I hope you find lots to love here too.

THANKS

It was so special to create a book that celebrates Australian food. I couldn't have done it alone however and there is an endless list of people I'm grateful to. Firstly, thank you to my long time friend, stylist and chef Emma Knowles, who I have known now for over 25 years. She went above and beyond. Also, a huge thanks to my business manager, Pip Sheldon, for her tireless efforts and ability to always pull everything together. Many people have been involved in this book, but without these two it most certainly wouldn't have happened.

I'd like to thank all of my staff, especially my team of chefs. I'm always thankful for their passion, hard work and sheer dedication to the job. I feel lucky to have such an incredible team.

A huge thanks to everyone at Murdoch, in particular Jane Morrow, Madeleine Kane, Katie Bosher and editor Kay Halsey. Thank you for a great collaboration. Thanks as well to talented photographer Will Meppem and to designers Jacqui Porter and Dan Peterson of Northwood Green.

I'm especially thankful to my business partner Bruce Solomon and of course my wonderful family, Sarah, Harry and Amelia, for their support and for giving me the freedom to do what I love.

Special thanks to my suppliers and all the farmers, growers and producers out there. I've always said that we chefs are only as good as the quality of the ingredients we use so I cannot thank you enough for all your hard work in bringing us the best. We couldn't do it without you.

Last, but not least, thanks to you and everyone who has bought my cookbooks, dined at my restaurants or simply enjoyed my food over the years.

Happy cooking,
Matt

PART ONE

COAST

COAST

The way I cook at home on the coast is very much driven by time – or to be more accurate, the lack of it. I know I'm not alone on this front. Running restaurants combined with family life can be challenging, but cooking at home, be it for family or friends, is the anchor. It's impossible to overstate the importance of sharing a meal with loved ones, especially a home-cooked one – it's a chance to re-connect and re-fuel, and not just in the physical sense.

Whether it's a quick weeknight meal, or more leisurely cooking for friends on the weekend, for me it's mostly about quick, easy and crowd-pleasing, with an emphasis on fresh flavours and a simple approach.

I have a compact vegetable garden at home, so whatever is growing well and abundantly often drives what I'm cooking – we eat a lot of salads at my place! Living on the coast also means easy access to great-quality seafood, so that's often a focus too. I even have a four-metre tinny that I sometimes take out into the little bay near home and catch squid – not nearly as often as I'd like to, to be honest!

It's fair to say that I'm a committed carnivore, and if I'm cooking meat, I'll focus on quality grass-fed meat, using cuts that lend themselves to speedy cooking (for the most part I leave the slow-cooking for when I'm at the farm).

Many of these recipes are my weeknight go-tos, while others are for casual weekend entertaining. You'll find dishes for breezy summer days and cooler nights, kick-starting breakfasts and sweets to hit the spot. Most of all, you'll find flavour and freshness, and lots of it. Isn't this how we love to eat by the Australian coast?

Preparation Time 15 minutes | **Cooking Time** 7 minutes | **Serves** 4

CRUSHED AVOCADO, SOFT EGGS and CHILLI-LIME SALT

It's pretty rare to see a breakfast menu in Australia that doesn't feature smashed avocado in one form or another. I could eat it almost every day without getting sick of it, but the key is to add loads of extra flavour to the avo – mine has plenty of lime, salty feta and an extra kick with a chilli-lime salt seasoning. Either poached or soft-boiled eggs make this an incredibly satisfying start to the day.

4 eggs, at room temperature
2 avocados
50 g ($1\frac{3}{4}$ oz) feta cheese, coarsely crumbled
2 tablespoons extra-virgin olive oil
Juice of 2 limes
200 g (7 oz) cherry tomatoes, coarsely chopped
1 small French shallot, finely diced
2 tablespoons coarsely chopped coriander (cilantro) leaves
Sourdough toast, to serve

CHILLI-LIME SALT

1 tablespoon sea salt
$\frac{1}{2}$ teaspoon chilli flakes
Finely grated zest of 1 lime

To make the chilli-lime salt, combine the ingredients in a bowl and set aside.

Bring a saucepan of water to the boil, add the eggs and boil for 7 minutes for soft yolks, then drain.

While the eggs are cooking, halve the avocados, remove the seed, scoop the flesh out of their skins into a bowl and coarsely mash with a fork, making sure you keep a bit of texture. Stir in the feta, half the olive oil, half the lime juice and season generously.

Combine the tomatoes, shallot, coriander and remaining oil in a separate bowl and add the remaining lime juice, to taste.

To serve, pile the crushed avocado on the toast. Break the eggs in half, scoop out of their shells and on top of the avocado. Spoon over the tomato dressing and serve seasoned with chilli-lime salt.

COCONUT-CHIA GRANOLA with TROPICAL FRUITS and COCONUT YOGHURT

Home-made granola is the best – you can play around with the combination of nuts and seeds, and also tailor the sweetness to suit yourself. In summer, I love it topped with tropical fruits and a dollop of coconut yoghurt for cool smoothness. It's a pantry stand-by for those in-a-hurry mid-week breakfasts, or even an on-the-go snack to be eaten by the handful.

COCONUT-CHIA GRANOLA

140 g (5 oz/$2\frac{1}{2}$ cups) coconut flakes

120 g ($4\frac{1}{4}$ oz) mixed nuts, such as almonds, pistachios and hazelnuts, coarsely chopped

100 g ($3\frac{1}{2}$ oz/1 cup) rolled (porridge) oats

100 g ($3\frac{1}{2}$ oz/1 cup) rolled barley (flakes)

60 g ($2\frac{1}{4}$ oz/$\frac{1}{3}$ cup) chia seeds

50 g ($1\frac{3}{4}$ oz/$\frac{1}{3}$ cup) pepitas (pumpkin seeds)

50 g ($1\frac{3}{4}$ oz/$\frac{1}{3}$ cup) sunflower seeds

50 g ($1\frac{3}{4}$ oz/$\frac{1}{3}$ cup) roasted buckwheat (kasha)

2 teaspoons ground cinnamon

1 teaspoon sea salt

80 ml ($2\frac{1}{2}$ fl oz/$\frac{1}{3}$ cup) coconut oil

80 g ($2\frac{3}{4}$ oz/$\frac{1}{4}$ cup) honey

2 teaspoons vanilla extract

TO SERVE

Coconut yoghurt

2 bananas, peeled and cut into chunks

1 mango, peeled and thickly sliced

$\frac{1}{2}$ small pineapple, peeled and cut into chunks

2 passionfruit

Finely grated zest of 1 lime

Honey

Lime wedges (optional)

To make the coconut-chia granola, preheat the oven to 150°C (300°F). Combine the dry ingredients in a large bowl. Melt the coconut oil, honey and vanilla in a small saucepan over a low heat, add to the dry ingredients, mix well to combine, then spread on large baking trays lined with baking paper and bake, stirring occasionally, for 20–25 minutes until golden brown. Cool completely on the trays, then store in an airtight jar or container for up to 2 weeks. Makes about 750 g (1 lb 10 oz).

To serve, pour the granola into bowls, top with a generous dollop of coconut yoghurt and arrange the banana, mango and pineapple on top. Spoon over the passion fruit pulp, scatter with lime zest, then drizzle with a little honey and serve with lime wedges, if using. You could also serve the granola with milk, if you like.

ALMOND MILK PORRIDGE with DATES, PECANS and MAPLE SYRUP

Porridge is one of the best starts to the day that you can have, and this dairy-free version is no exception. Using almond milk gives a lighter finish, but the end result is just as satisfying. I've made my own almond milk here as I like that there are none of the hidden preservatives, oils or sugars that are often found in store-bought almond milk, but if you can get your hands on a good cold-pressed nut milk, feel free to use it instead. Make sure you use traditional rolled (porridge) oats, not the quick-cook ones, or you won't get the lovely creamy texture.

200 g (7 oz/2 cups) rolled (porridge) oats
½ cinnamon stick
50 g (1¾ oz/¼ cup) Medjool dates, pitted
    and coarsely chopped
50 g (1¾ oz/½ cup) pecans, toasted
    and chopped
60 ml (2 fl oz/¼ cup) maple syrup

ALMOND MILK

200 g (7 oz/1¼ cups) almonds, skin on
2 teaspoons ground linseed (flaxseed)

To make the almond milk, place the almonds in a bowl and top up with enough water to cover by a few centimetres. Refrigerate overnight, then drain and discard the water. Transfer to a blender, add the ground linseed and 1 litre (35 fl oz/4 cups) water and blend for 2–3 minutes until smooth. Strain through a sieve lined with a double layer of muslin (cheesecloth) into a bowl, allowing the mixture to drain for 15–20 minutes, then gather up the muslin and squeeze the almond solids to extract as much almond milk as possible (the more liquid you squeeze out, the richer your almond milk will be). This will make about 1 litre (35 fl oz/4 cups). Refrigerate in a sterilised bottle for up to 3 days.

To make the porridge, combine the rolled oats, cinnamon, 700 ml (24 fl oz/2¾ cups) almond milk and a pinch of sea salt in a saucepan over low–medium heat and bring gently to a simmer. Simmer, stirring occasionally, for 5–6 minutes until the oats become creamy. If the porridge becomes too thick, add a little more almond milk. Discard the cinnamon and serve the porridge scattered with dates and pecans and drizzled with maple syrup.

EXCELLENT OMELETTE

I reckon knowing how to make an omelette is an excellent life skill (it's also an excellent test of a chef's skills) – it really is the answer to almost any food-based indecision as it's just as good for lunch, dinner or supper as it is for breakfast. Once you master the technique, the fillings are up to you.

80 g (2¾ oz/⅓ cup) butter, diced
1 spring onion (scallion), thinly sliced
1 garlic clove, finely crushed
100 g (3½ oz/1 cup) baby English spinach
3 eggs

20 g (¾ oz/¼ cup) finely grated parmesan
   cheese, plus extra to serve
Coarsely chopped flat-leaf (Italian)
   parsley leaves, to serve

Heat a third of the butter in a non-stick frying pan (about 20 cm/ 8 inches in diameter) over a medium–high heat until the butter foams. Add the spring onion and garlic and sauté for 1–2 minutes until tender, then add the spinach and toss quickly over the heat to wilt. Season and tip into a sieve to drain any excess liquid.

Wipe out your pan with paper towels, return to a medium heat and add the remaining butter. Quickly crack the eggs into a bowl, season and whisk with a fork (you just want to break the eggs up without incorporating too much air). When the butter is foaming, add the eggs to the pan, then as the omelette edges begin to set, slide a heatproof spatula under an edge, lifting and tilting the frying pan so the uncooked egg runs underneath – after about 45 seconds the eggs will be almost three-quarters cooked. Scatter with parmesan, then the spinach and cook for another 20 seconds, then tip the pan up and allow one side of the omelette to fall on to its opposite side. Slide the omelette out of the pan onto a serving plate and serve hot, scattered with extra parmesan and coarsely chopped parsley.

Preparation Time 20 minutes | **Serves** 4 as a side or light meal

WATERMELON and POMEGRANATE SALAD with WHIPPED FETA

I love the salty-sweet combo of this salad – it's the perfect cool down on a hot day. Pomegranate adds the most beautiful texture and tart flavour. The trick to getting the seeds out of a pomegranate easily is to roll it firmly on a bench before you break it open. This loosens the seeds from the membranes that hold them in place, making it much easier to get the little beauties out.

1 kg (2 lb 4 oz) seedless watermelon, peeled and cut into chunks
40 g (1½ oz/¼ cup) toasted almonds, coarsely chopped
Seeds from ½ pomegranate
1 small French shallot, thinly sliced
35 g (1¼ oz/1 cup) wild rocket (arugula)
1 large handful mint leaves
2½ tablespoons extra-virgin olive oil
1 tablespoon red wine vinegar
Finely grated zest and juice of ½ lemon, or to taste
½ small garlic clove, finely chopped
Sumac, for dusting

WHIPPED FETA

150 g (5½ oz) feta cheese
2 tablespoons olive oil
Finely grated zest and juice of ½ lemon
½ small garlic clove

To make the whipped feta, blend the ingredients in a blender or small food processor until smooth, season to taste and spread over a serving platter.

Arrange the watermelon over the whipped feta and scatter with the almonds, pomegranate and shallot, then with the rocket and mint leaves.

Whisk the olive oil, vinegar, lemon zest, juice and garlic in a bowl to combine, season to taste and drizzle over the salad. Scatter with sumac and serve.

BUTTER LETTUCE with GOAT'S CHEESE, PEAS and PRESERVED LEMON

I reckon butter lettuce is underrated – I love to combine its tender leaves with crunchier cos, along with spring vegetables such as freshly podded peas and broad beans. Preserved lemons add a distinctive salty tang to the salad.

100 g ($3\frac{1}{2}$ oz/$\frac{2}{3}$ cup) podded peas
  (about 300 g/$10\frac{1}{2}$ oz unpodded)
100 g ($3\frac{1}{2}$ oz/$\frac{1}{2}$ cup) podded broad beans
  (about 350 g/12 oz unpodded)
3 preserved lemon quarters, rinsed
2 butter lettuces, outer leaves discarded
2 baby cos lettuces, outer leaves
  discarded

1 large handful mint leaves
100 g ($3\frac{1}{2}$ oz) goat's cheese
60 ml (2 fl oz/$\frac{1}{4}$ cup) lemon-pressed
  olive oil (see note)
Juice of 1 lemon, or to taste

Blanch the peas and beans together in a saucepan of boiling salted water for just 2–3 minutes until tender, then drain and refresh in iced water. Drain again, then peel the skins from the broad beans.

Use a small, sharp knife to cut the pulp from the preserved lemons and discard, then thinly slice the rind into strips.

Separate the lettuce leaves and tear some of the larger ones into pieces, then cut the hearts of the cos in half. Wash in a large bowl of water, drain well and arrange in a serving bowl. Scatter with

peas, broad beans, preserved lemon and mint, then crumble the goat's cheese over the top.

Whisk the lemon oil and lemon juice in a separate bowl to combine, season to taste, then drizzle over the salad to serve.

NOTE Lemon-pressed olive oil is made by cold-pressing halved lemons and olives together to create an olive oil infused with lemon flavour. You can buy this oil at many delicatessens and some supermarkets.

FIG SALAD with GOAT'S CURD

This salad is all about making perfectly ripe figs the hero – be sure to have your figs at room temperature, as serving them chilled will dull their flavour. Goat's curd adds a soft and subtle flavour here. It's available from delicatessens and specialty cheese stores, but if you can't find it, you could use marinated feta or even labne, if you like.

$\frac{1}{2}$ loaf of ciabatta
125 ml (4 fl oz/$\frac{1}{2}$ cup) olive oil
1 tablespoon red wine vinegar
2 teaspoons honey
1 teaspoon wholegrain mustard

6 black figs
200 g (7 oz) goat's curd
100 g (3$\frac{1}{2}$ oz) mixed salad leaves
Basil leaves, to serve

Preheat the oven to 180°C (350°F).

To make croutons, thickly slice the ciabatta and tear into rough 1 cm ($\frac{1}{2}$ inch) pieces. Toss in a bowl with half the olive oil, season to taste, then spread on a baking tray and bake for 6–7 minutes until golden brown and crunchy. Set aside to cool.

To make the dressing, whisk the vinegar, honey, mustard and remaining olive oil in a bowl to combine and season to taste.

Cut the figs into wedges or tear into halves and arrange on a plate. Dollop with the goat's curd, scatter with mixed leaves, the croutons and basil, then drizzle with the dressing and serve.

BURRATA with BROAD BEANS and MINT

Burrata is one of the most amazing cheeses – a pouch of mozzarella filled with a mixture of soft curd and cream. When you break into it, the creamy insides mingle and mix with the broad bean dressing to create the most beautiful dish. Crusty sourdough bread is excellent served alongside to mop it all up.

500 g (1 lb 2 oz) broad beans in the pod
Finely grated zest and juice of 1 lemon, or to taste

100 ml ($3\frac{1}{2}$ fl oz) olive oil
4 burrata (see note)
Torn mint leaves, to serve

Bring a large saucepan of salted water to the boil over high heat, add the broad beans and boil for a minute or two until bright green and just tender. Drain and plunge into iced water to stop the cooking process. Drain and peel away the outer shells, then combine in a bowl with the lemon zest and olive oil. Squeeze in the lemon juice to taste, then season.

Place a burrata in the centre of each serving plate, spoon over the broad beans and dressing, scatter with mint and serve.

NOTE Burrata is available from many delicatessens and specialty cheese shops. If it's unavailable, you could use buffalo mozzarella instead.

ROAST ASPARAGUS with PARMESAN CRUMBS and SOFT EGG

When asparagus is in season, I love making it a hero. While this dish could be considered a side, it's also substantial enough to serve as a light meal. Sometimes I make this dish using buttery brioche crumbs instead of sourdough crumbs, which adds a beautiful richness.

600 g (1 lb 5 oz) asparagus
  (about 4 bunches), trimmed
2 tablespoons olive oil
75 ml (2½ fl oz) extra-virgin olive oil
2 teaspoons Dijon mustard
Juice of ½ lemon, or to taste
1 tablespoon sherry vinegar
6 soft-boiled eggs, peeled
Finely grated parmesan cheese, to serve
Coarsely chopped flat-leaf (Italian)
  parsley, mint and thyme leaves
  (optional), to serve

PARMESAN CRUMBS
75 g (2½ oz) coarse sourdough
  breadcrumbs
30 g (1 oz/⅓ cup) finely grated
  parmesan cheese
2 teaspoons each finely chopped
  thyme and parsley leaves
1 garlic clove, finely chopped
75 ml (2½ fl oz) olive oil

To make the parmesan crumbs, preheat the oven to 180°C (350°F). Combine the breadcrumbs, parmesan, herbs, garlic and olive oil in a bowl, season and stir to evenly combine. Spread on a baking tray and bake, stirring occasionally so the crumbs colour evenly, for 10–12 minutes until golden brown.

Increase the oven temperature to 220°C (425°F). Spread the asparagus in a single layer on a baking tray, drizzle with the olive oil, season and roast for 5–6 minutes until just tender. Meanwhile, whisk the extra-virgin olive oil, mustard, lemon juice and vinegar in a bowl to combine and season. Thin with a little cold water if necessary to give a drizzling consistency.

Transfer the roast asparagus to plates, crumble over the soft-boiled eggs and drizzle with the mustard dressing. Grate over plenty of parmesan and serve scattered with parmesan crumbs and herbs.

SALMON GRAVLAX

Curing is one of my favourite ways to enjoy the incredibly good-quality fish we're lucky enough to get here in Australia. You'll often find cured fish on the menu in various forms at Chiswick, ARIA and, of course, North Bondi Fish. Curing allows the natural flavours of the fish to shine through and it works well with almost any fish, although the oiliness of salmon is a no-brainer. I'll often make this if I'm having friends around for lunch and if there are any leftovers (unlikely!) I'll use the rest for brekky with scrambled eggs.

20 g ($\frac{3}{4}$ oz/$\frac{1}{4}$ cup) coriander seeds
50 g (1$\frac{3}{4}$ oz/$\frac{1}{3}$ cup) black peppercorns
250 g (9 oz/$\frac{3}{4}$ cup) rock salt
75 g (2$\frac{1}{2}$ oz/$\frac{1}{3}$ cup) caster
    (superfine) sugar
1 small fennel bulb, coarsely chopped
1 lemon, coarsely chopped

1 side of salmon (about 1.3 kg/3 lb),
    skin-on, pin-boned
1 tablespoon Dijon mustard
1 bunch coarsely chopped dill
Lemon wedges, crème fraîche and crusty
    bread, to serve

Place the coriander seeds in a small dry frying pan and dry-roast over a medium–high heat, shaking the pan occasionally, for a minute or two until fragrant. Tip into a mortar and pestle, add the peppercorns and coarsely crush.

Combine the rock salt, sugar, fennel, lemon and crushed spices in a food processor and process to a paste.

Line a baking tray or dish large enough to hold the salmon flat with plastic wrap, then spread out half the salt mixture on the plastic wrap. Score the skin side of the salmon with a sharp knife, four to five times about 5 mm ($\frac{1}{4}$ inch) deep, then place skin-side down on top of the salt mixture. Spread the remaining salt mixture over the flesh of the salmon, wrap tightly in the plastic wrap, then in another layer of plastic wrap to prevent any leaks

(as the salmon cures the curing mixture will turn into a liquid while the moisture is drawn from the fish). Place back in the tray or dish and refrigerate for 24 hours. Turn the salmon over in the tray and refrigerate for another 24 hours to continue curing.

Unwrap the salmon and wipe off any excess curing mixture, lightly rinse under cold running water, then pat dry with paper towels. Brush the flesh of the salmon with the mustard, then scatter with the dill, lightly pressing to help it stick to the fish. Eat immediately or wrap in a fresh piece of plastic wrap and refrigerate for up to 5 days.

To serve, thinly slice the salmon with a very sharp knife across the grain of the fish and serve with lemon wedges, crème fraîche and crusty bread.

PORK and PRAWN SUNG CHOI BAO

One of the things I love most about Australian food is that it's such a mix of influences and flavours, thanks to the many migrant groups who have made Australia their home. Chinese restaurants can be found from coast to coast and everywhere in between, so it's not surprising we've embraced these flavours. I wouldn't call this a traditional sung choi bao as I've added prawns to give it a surf 'n' turf remix, but it sure is tasty. I love the casual nature of it – roll, eat and lick fingers!

2–3 tablespoons vegetable oil
3 spring onions (scallions), thinly sliced
10 g ($\frac{1}{4}$ oz) fresh ginger, peeled and finely grated
3 garlic cloves, finely chopped
1 small red chilli, seeds removed, finely chopped
500 g (1 lb 2 oz) minced pork neck (ask your butcher)
8 raw prawns (shrimp), peeled, deveined and coarsely chopped
1 tablespoon tamari

1 tablespoon fish sauce
Juice of 1 lime
2 teaspoons caster (superfine) sugar
1 small carrot, cut into julienne
50 g ($1\frac{3}{4}$ oz) snow peas, trimmed and cut into julienne
115 g (4 oz/1 cup) bean sprouts, tails trimmed
1 handful coriander (cilantro) leaves
1 handful mint leaves
8 basil leaves
8 iceberg lettuce leaves

Heat the vegetable oil in a wok over a high heat, add the spring onions, ginger, garlic and chilli and stir-fry for 1 minute until fragrant. Add the pork and prawns, stir-fry for a minute or two until almost cooked through, then add the tamari, fish sauce, lime juice and caster sugar and simmer for a minute.

Add the carrot and snow peas, stir-fry for 1–2 minutes until just tender, then remove from the heat and toss through the bean sprouts and herbs. Serve spooned into the lettuce cups.

LAMB CUTLETS with DUKKAH
and TAHINI SAUCE

Lamb cutlets are usually thought of as a main meal, but they're also perfect for a stand-up casual snack. They've got a built-in handle too, making them easy to eat with a drink in hand, which is why they're food I eat at home on the coast. The dukkah spice mix adds beautiful fragrance and texture. It makes more than you'll need, but you can use it on almost anything – think barbecued chicken or fish, or use in the traditional way and dip fresh crusty bread into olive oil then the dukkah.

12 lamb cutlets
Torn mint leaves and lemon wedges,
    to serve

DUKKAH
1 teaspoon cumin seeds
1 teaspoon coriander seeds
1 teaspoon fennel seeds
1 teaspoon black peppercorns
2 tablespoons toasted hazelnuts,
    finely chopped

1 tablespoon sesame seeds
1 teaspoon sea salt
1 teaspoon sumac

TAHINI SAUCE
200 g (7 oz/$\frac{3}{4}$ cup) Greek-style yoghurt
2 tablespoons tahini
2 tablespoons lemon juice
1 garlic clove, crushed

Preheat a barbecue or chargrill pan to a medium–high heat for 15 minutes.

Meanwhile, to make the dukkah combine the whole spices in a dry frying pan and dry-roast, stirring occasionally so they toast evenly, for a minute or two until fragrant. Cool slightly, grind in a mortar and pestle, then combine in a bowl with the remaining ingredients. The dukkah will keep in an airtight container for up to 1 month.

To make the tahini sauce, stir the ingredients in a bowl until smooth and combined and season to taste.

Season the lamb cutlets and barbecue, turning once, for about 4–5 minutes until browned and cooked medium-rare. Set aside to rest for 2 minutes, then serve scattered with dukkah and mint, along with the tahini sauce and lemon wedges.

LEMONY FISH BROTH

This chunky, rustic broth is light, yet very satisfying. Use a mixture of fish –
I like to add some salmon or trout to the mix and whatever firm-fleshed white
fish is good on the day. You could even add mussels, if you wanted to. Crusty
bread is the best accompaniment here to dip into this moreish broth.

2 tablespoons olive oil
1 tablespoon butter, diced
1 leek, coarsely chopped
1 small fennel bulb, coarsely chopped,
    fronds reserved to serve
2 garlic cloves, finely chopped
2 floury potatoes, such as Sebago (about
    500 g/1 lb 2 oz), coarsely chopped
200 ml (7 fl oz) dry white wine
1 litre (35 fl oz/4 cups) fish or
    chicken stock

3 thyme sprigs
1 small fresh bay leaf
300 g (10½ oz) skinless firm white fish
    fillets, such as cod, blue eye trevalla or
    gemfish, cut into bite-sized pieces
Finely grated zest and juice of 1 lemon,
    or to taste
Coarsely chopped dill and flat-leaf
    (Italian) parsley leaves, to serve

Heat the olive oil and butter in a large saucepan over a medium–high heat until the butter foams. Add the leek, fennel and garlic and sauté, stirring occasionally, for 5–6 minutes until the vegetables are tender and translucent. Add the potatoes and cook, stirring occasionally for a minute or two, then add the wine and boil for 2–3 minutes until almost evaporated.

Add the stock, thyme and bay leaf, bring to a simmer, reduce the heat to medium and simmer for 12–15 minutes until the potatoes begin to break down. Discard the thyme and bay leaf, then remove two-thirds of the potatoes from the broth with a slotted spoon.

Blend the remaining broth with a hand-held blender until half-puréed, then return the potatoes back to the pan. Add the fish and gently poach for 2–3 minutes until just cooked through – don't boil. Stir through the lemon zest and juice, check the seasoning and serve hot, scattered with dill, parsley and the fennel fronds.

FARRO, PEA and LETTUCE SALAD with CHARRED LEMON DRESSING

Salads don't have to be light and delicate – you can make them into a satisfying meal in their own right by adding lentils or grains like barley or farro. Farro is an ancient type of wheat with a great nutty flavour and texture, which works perfectly with the sweetness of the peas. You can buy farro at delicatessens and health food stores. If it's unavailable, you could use coarse burghul or even barley instead.

300 g (10½ oz) farro
200 g (7 oz/1⅓ cups) podded peas or frozen peas
200 g (7 oz) sugar snap peas, trimmed
1 bunch asparagus, trimmed and cut into rough 4 cm (1½ inch) pieces
1 large handful coarsely torn flat-leaf (Italian) parsley leaves
1 large handful coarsely torn mint leaves
3 spring onions (scallions), thinly sliced

2 baby cos lettuces, outer leaves removed and coarsely torn, hearts cut into quarters
Olive oil, for drizzling

CHARRED LEMON DRESSING
½ small lemon, ends trimmed, halved
90 ml (3 fl oz) extra-virgin olive oil
1 tablespoon sherry vinegar, or to taste
½ garlic clove
Pinch of sugar

Cook the farro in a saucepan of boiling water for 20–25 minutes until tender, then drain and spread on a tray to cool. Cook the peas, sugar snaps and asparagus in a separate saucepan of boiling salted water for 2–3 minutes or until just tender, then drain and refresh under cold running water. Drain well and combine in a bowl with the farro, herbs and spring onion and season.

Meanwhile, to make the charred lemon dressing preheat a barbecue or chargrill pan to a medium–high heat. Chargrill the lemon quarters, turning occasionally, for 6–8 minutes until tender and lightly charred. Discard the seeds, then coarsely chop the lemon and process in a small food processor with the remaining ingredients to a rough dressing. Thin to a drizzling consistency with a little cold water if necessary. Season to taste and set aside.

Drizzle the lettuce with a little oil and on the barbecue or chargrill pan, still over a medium–high heat, cook, turning occasionally, for 2–3 minutes until charred and slightly wilted. Add to the farro mixture, drizzle with the dressing to taste and toss to combine.

TANGY GREEN and WHITE SLAW

I reckon no barbecue lunch is complete without a great slaw. To my mind, it should be crisp and crunchy, so I get all the raw ingredients prepped and the dressing made, then toss them all together just before serving. While a lot of people think a slaw has to be all about the cabbage, I've added a bit of shaved broccoli to the mix too, along with tart green apple, to add little pockets of different texture and flavour. A mandolin to slice the veggies makes short work of the prep – if you don't have one, I recommend you buy one. They're worth every penny!

1 small head of broccoli
(about 300 g/10½ oz)
¼ small white cabbage
(about 500 g/1 lb 2 oz)
2 Granny Smith apples
1 teaspoon lemon juice
3 spring onions (scallions), thinly sliced
1 large handful torn flat-leaf (Italian)
parsley leaves, plus extra to serve
1 large handful torn mint leaves,
plus extra to serve

BUTTERMILK DRESSING
60 g (2¼ oz/¼ cup) mayonnaise
1 tablespoon apple cider vinegar
1 tablespoon lemon juice
Finely grated zest of ½ lemon
1 garlic clove, finely grated
100 ml (3½ fl oz) buttermilk
60 ml (2 fl oz/¼ cup) extra-virgin olive oil

Cut the thick base off the broccoli and discard, then cut the broccoli into florets. Shave the tops of the florets on a mandolin into a bowl, then shave the stalks too.

Thinly shave the cabbage using the mandolin into the bowl. Cut the apples into matchsticks on the mandolin and toss in the lemon juice to prevent discolouring. Add the apple, spring onion and herbs to the bowl and toss to combine.

To make the buttermilk dressing, whisk the mayonnaise, vinegar, lemon juice, lemon zest and garlic in a bowl until smooth, then add the buttermilk and olive oil and whisk until combined. Season to taste.

To serve, drizzle the buttermilk dressing over the salad to taste, toss to lightly coat and combine, then serve scattered with the extra herbs.

BABY CORN with DILL and PINE NUTS

This cracking dish is on the menu at Chiswick when corn is at its best. I love the unusual combination of dill and pine nuts with the lime and chilli, but the sweetness of the corn is the real star here.

1 tablespoon pine nuts
Kernels from 1 corn cob, blanched
2 tablespoon coarsely chopped dill
Finely grated zest and juice of 1 lime
1 tablespoon vegetable oil
1 tablespoon olive oil
120 g ($4\frac{1}{4}$ oz) baby corn

SRIRACHA DRESSING
1 tablespoon mayonnaise
$\frac{1}{4}$ teaspoon Tabasco sauce
$\frac{1}{2}$ teaspoon sriracha sauce

Heat a small frying pan over a medium–high heat, add the pine nuts and dry-roast, shaking the pan often, for 2–3 minutes until golden brown, then transfer to a bowl to cool. Add the corn kernels, dill and lime zest and season.

To make the dressing, mix the mayonnaise, Tabasco, sriracha and lime juice in a bowl to combine and season to taste.

Combine the vegetable oil and the olive oil in a frying pan over a medium–high heat, add the baby corn and fry, turning occasionally, for 3–4 minutes until tender and golden brown all over. Drain on paper towels, season to taste and combine with the sriracha dressing. Serve topped with the corn, dill and pine nuts.

TOMATO SALAD with QUICK-PICKLED ONION and BASIL DRESSING

Tomatoes and basil are one of the most classic food marriages and it's hard to go wrong when you put these two together. I use a variety of large heirloom tomatoes and cherry tomatoes to get a good mix of shape and colour, but the key is to make sure they're perfectly ripe and at room temperature. The quick-pickled onions used here are a great fridge staple – you can use them in 3 hours, but they will last a couple of weeks. I also use them on burgers, alongside a barbecued steak, tucked into a sandwich or even through my killer potato salad (see page 164).

1 large handful basil leaves, plus extra
    to serve
$\frac{1}{2}$ small garlic clove
80 ml ($2\frac{1}{2}$ fl oz/$\frac{1}{3}$ cup) extra-virgin olive oil
Juice of $\frac{1}{2}$ lemon, or to taste
4 large heirloom tomatoes, thickly sliced
    or cut into wedges
200 g (7 oz) mixed cherry tomatoes,
    halved or thickly sliced

QUICK-PICKLED ONION

1 small red onion, sliced into 3 mm
    ($\frac{1}{8}$ inch) thick rounds
1 garlic clove, peeled and halved
1 small red chilli, split in half
185 ml (6 fl oz/$\frac{3}{4}$ cup) white wine vinegar
1 teaspoon caster (superfine) sugar
1 teaspoon sea salt
$\frac{1}{2}$ teaspoon coarsely cracked
    black peppercorns

To make the quick-pickled onion, separate the onion slices into rings, place in a sieve over the sink and slowly pour over hot water from a just-boiled kettle to blanch. Drain well, then place in a sterilised glass jar along with the garlic and chilli. Stir the vinegar, sugar, salt and peppercorns in a jug to dissolve, pour over the onions to cover completely, then seal and refrigerate for at least 3 hours and up to 2 weeks.

Combine the basil, garlic and a good pinch of sea salt in a mortar and pestle and pound to a rough paste. Add the olive oil and lemon juice to taste, pound to combine, then season to taste.

Arrange the tomatoes on a platter and scatter with some extra basil leaves. Drain some of the quick-pickled onion and scatter over the tomatoes, then drizzle with the basil dressing.

GRILLED CALAMARI
with SALSA VERDE

Squid can be a misunderstood creature – too often it's overcooked
and rubbery, which is less than appealing. But if it's super-fresh and cooked
quickly over a very high heat, it's sweet and tender. I sometimes catch it in
the bay near home, and this is my favourite way to cook it. I love to serve this
tangy salsa verde alongside as it has a subtle brininess that works perfectly
with the calamari.

2 large squid (calamari) (about 250 g/
    9 oz each), cleaned
2 tablespoons olive oil
Lemon wedges, to serve

SALSA VERDE
30 g (1 oz/2 cups) flat-leaf (Italian) parsley
    leaves (2 bunches)

200 ml (7 fl oz) olive oil
2 teaspoons salted capers,
    rinsed and drained
4 cornichons
2 anchovies
1 garlic clove, finely chopped
Juice of 1 lemon

To make the salsa verde, combine the ingredients in a blender, season to taste and blitz for a minute or two until very smooth, then check the seasoning and adjust if necessary.

To prepare the calamari, heat a chargrill pan or barbecue to a high heat. Score the inside of the calamari with a sharp knife in a crisscross pattern and cut into bite-sized pieces. Place in a bowl, season and toss with olive oil. Grill for a minute on each side until golden brown and just cooked through, then serve drizzled with the salsa verde with lemon wedges to squeeze over.

FISH TACOS

I remember when tacos first came into the general consciousness in
Australia when I was a kid – it was all about mince flavoured with premade
spice mixes and sauces from a taco kit. Tacos are still popular at my place,
but these days it's about soft tortillas, tangy home-made salsas and
crisp fried fish.

Vegetable oil, for deep-frying
400 g (14 oz) skinless firm white fish
    fillets, cut into bite-sized pieces
Seasoned plain (all-purpose) flour,
    for dusting
6 white corn tortillas
150 g (5½ oz) white cabbage, shredded
Coriander (cilantro) leaves, lime wedges
    and pickled jalapeño chillies, to serve

TOMATO SALSA
2 tomatoes, diced
2 spring onions (scallions), thinly sliced
1 fresh jalapeño chilli, finely chopped
1 garlic clove, finely chopped
1 small handful coriander (cilantro)
    leaves, finely chopped

Juice of 1 lime
2 tablespoons olive oil
Pinch of ground cumin

SOUR CREAM SAUCE
200 ml (7 fl oz) sour cream
60 g (2¼ oz/¼ cup) Greek-style yoghurt
Juice of 1 lime
Ground chilli, to taste

BATTER
1 egg
150 g (5½ oz/1 cup) plain
    (all-purpose) flour
½ teaspoon bicarbonate of soda
    (baking soda)

To make the tomato salsa, combine the ingredients in a bowl,
season to taste and set aside.

To make the sour cream sauce, mix the ingredients in a bowl
until smooth and combined, season to taste and set aside.

Preheat the oil in a deep-fat fryer or large saucepan to 200°C
(400°F). To make the batter, whisk the egg until light and fluffy,
then fold in the flour, bicarbonate of soda and 250 ml (9 fl oz/
1 cup) iced water (the batter should be a thin consistency – add
a little extra water if necessary). Season.

Dust the flathead pieces in the seasoned flour, then dip into
the batter, shaking off any excess, and carefully deep-fry in

batches (be careful as hot oil will spit), turning occasionally, for
2–3 minutes until light golden and crisp. Drain on paper towels
and season to taste.

Heat a frying pan over a high heat and warm the tortillas in the
pan for a minute on each side. Wrap loosely in a clean tea towel
while you cook the remaining tortillas.

To serve, fill each taco with some fried fish and shredded
cabbage, top with the salsa and sour cream sauce and serve with
a scattering of coriander, lime wedges and jalapeños.

ROAST TOMATO and GARLIC SOUP

This is one of the simplest soups going around, but it's so full of flavour. It's pretty great on its own, but I reckon it's even better served with some cheesy toast for dipping.

2 kg (4 lb 8 oz) very ripe
    tomatoes, halved
4 long red chillies, halved lengthways
2 red onions, cut into wedges
1 red capsicum (pepper), seeds removed
    and cut into wedges
1 head of garlic, halved

3 tablespoons olive oil
2 x 400 g (14 oz) tins of plum tomatoes
500 ml (17 fl oz/2 cups) vegetable stock
2 tablespoons balsamic vinegar,
    or to taste
Torn basil and oregano and extra-virgin
    olive oil, to serve

Preheat the oven to 200°C (400°F). Combine the tomatoes, chilli, onion, capsicum and garlic in a large roasting tin (or two smaller roasting tins), drizzle with the olive oil, season to taste and roast for 50–55 minutes until very tender.

When cool enough to handle, squeeze the garlic from their skins (discard the skins). Tip the vegetables, garlic and pan juices into a large saucepan, add the tinned tomatoes and vegetable stock, bring to a simmer and cook for 4–5 minutes for the flavours to combine. Add the vinegar, then blitz with a hand-held blender until very smooth and season to taste.

Serve hot, scattered with herbs and drizzled with extra-virgin olive oil.

OVEN-BAKED FISH and CHIPS

I love fish and chips when it's done well, and when it came to the fish and chips on the menu at North Bondi Fish, I was a stickler for getting it right. This oven-baked version is the next best thing and surprisingly easy. Serve with mayo or tartare sauce for dipping and a crisp green salad for a fresh and crunchy contrast.

1 kg (2 lb 4 oz) floury potatoes, such as Sebago, scrubbed and cut into 5 mm ($\frac{1}{4}$ inch) thick chips
90 ml (3 fl oz) olive oil
120 g ($4\frac{1}{4}$ oz/2 cups) panko crumbs
2 teaspoons finely chopped thyme leaves
1 garlic clove, finely chopped
Finely grated zest of $\frac{1}{2}$ lemon, plus lemon wedges to serve

2 eggs
1 tablespoon Dijon mustard
Seasoned plain (all-purpose) flour, for dusting
500 g (1 lb 2 oz) skinless flathead, snapper or other firm white fish fillets, cut into rough 10 cm (4 inch) pieces

Preheat the oven to 240°C (475°F) and place a baking tray in the oven on the top rack. Toss the potatoes and two-thirds of the olive oil in a bowl to evenly coat the potato, season, then spread in a single layer on the baking tray. Bake, tossing occasionally, for 20–25 minutes while you prepare the fish.

To prepare the fish, heat the remaining oil in a frying pan over a medium–high heat, add the crumbs, thyme, garlic and lemon zest and toast for 1–2 minutes until crisp and light golden, then tip onto a plate and season.

Whisk the eggs and mustard in a bowl to combine and place the seasoned flour in a separate bowl. Dust the fish in the flour, then dip into the egg mixture and toss into the crumbs, pressing so the crumbs stick evenly to the fish. Place the fish in a single layer on a well-oiled rack placed over a baking tray and put the fish on the middle rack of the oven. Bake for 6–8 minutes until the fish is just cooked through. Serve with the chips, lemon wedges, mayo or tartare sauce and a crisp green salad.

ROCKET PESTO with SPELT SPAGHETTINI

The peppery leaves of the rocket (arugula) give this pesto a real kick. I like to toss it through spelt spaghettini as it has an earthy, nutty flavour that pairs well with it. Alternatively, fresh pasta such as tagliarini would be amazing too.

150 g ($5\frac{1}{2}$ oz) rocket (arugula)
    (about 2 bunches), stalks trimmed
50 g ($1\frac{3}{4}$ oz/$2\frac{1}{2}$ cups) basil leaves,
    plus extra to serve
1 garlic clove
50 g ($1\frac{3}{4}$ oz/$\frac{1}{3}$ cup) toasted pine nuts

140 ml ($4\frac{1}{2}$ fl oz) olive oil
75 g ($2\frac{1}{2}$ oz/$\frac{3}{4}$ cup) finely grated
    parmesan cheese, plus extra to serve
Juice of $\frac{1}{2}$ lemon, or to taste
350 g (12 oz) spelt spaghettini

To make the rocket pesto, combine the rocket, basil, garlic, half the pine nuts and three-quarters of the olive oil in a blender, season and blend until smooth. Transfer to a container, stir in half the parmesan and the remaining oil, cover and refrigerate until required.

Just before serving, stir in the remaining pine nuts, add a squeeze of lemon to taste and check the seasoning.

Bring a large saucepan of salted water to the boil, add the spaghettini and boil until al dente – the exact time will depend on the pasta, but usually this will take 8–10 minutes. Drain, reserving a tablespoon or two of the pasta cooking water. Return the pasta to the pan, toss through the pesto and a little of the reserved cooking water and serve hot, scattered with extra basil and parmesan.

FELAFEL with TABBOULI and BEETROOT HUMMUS

Middle Eastern flavours have really found their way into modern Australian cooking – all those fragrant spices and punchy tastes are pretty irresistible. These felafel are an excellent snack as is, or you could wrap them up in pita bread with the hummus and salad for a more substantial meal. Pickled chillies would add a great extra hit of heat if you have them to hand.

200 g (7 oz/1 cup) dried chickpeas, soaked overnight in cold water, drained
70 g (2½ oz/¼ cup) tahini
2 tablespoons olive oil
2 garlic cloves, crushed
1 teaspoon ground cumin
½ teaspoon paprika
75 ml (2½ fl oz) lemon juice, plus extra lemon wedges to serve
Vegetable oil, for frying
Sumac, to serve

BEETROOT HUMMUS
200 g (7 oz/1 cup) dried chickpeas, soaked overnight in cold water, drained
80 ml (2½ fl oz/⅓ cup) lemon juice
2 tablespoons tahini
2 tablespoons extra-virgin olive oil
1 beetroot (beet), peeled and coarsely grated
1 garlic clove, coarsely chopped

TABBOULI
1 large handful each torn flat-leaf (Italian) parsley and mint leaves
½ small red onion, thinly sliced
1½ tablespoons extra-virgin olive oil
1 tablespoon lemon juice

To make the felafel, process the chickpeas, tahini, olive oil, garlic, cumin, paprika and lemon juice in a food processor for about 3–4 minutes until the mixture is finely chopped and holds its shape when pressed together. Season, transfer to a bowl, cover and refrigerate for 2 hours.

To make the beetroot hummus, boil the chickpeas in a saucepan of unsalted water for 25–30 minutes until tender, then drain (reserve a little of the cooking water) and transfer to a food processor. Add the remaining ingredients, season and process until smooth. Thin with a little of the reserved cooking liquid if necessary and set aside.

Preheat the vegetable oil in a deep-fat fryer or deep-sided saucepan to 170°C (325°F). Roll the falafel mixture into walnut-sized patties and deep-fry in batches, turning occasionally, for a minute or two until golden brown (be careful as the hot oil may spit). Drain on paper towels, season to taste and keep warm.

To make the tabbouli, combine the parsley, mint, onion, extra-virgin olive oil and lemon juice in a bowl, season to taste and toss to combine. Serve with the felafel and beetroot hummus, scattered with sumac and with lemon wedges to squeeze over.

ROASTED LAMB RACK with QUINOA SALAD and YOGHURT-TAHINI DRESSING

A rack of lamb makes a great centrepiece to a meal and it's pretty low-fuss too. The key to super-tender lamb is to give it a good rest before you serve it; as a rule, let it rest for about half the amount of time it was in the oven. Cover loosely with foil so it doesn't cool down too much.

2 x 9-cutlet lamb racks, fat scored in a crosshatch pattern, at room temperature
2 teaspoons ground cumin, plus extra to serve
1 tablespoon sea salt
1 tablespoon olive oil

QUINOA SALAD
250 g (9 oz) quinoa
300 g ($10\frac{1}{2}$ oz) cherry tomatoes, halved
1 Lebanese (short) cucumber, quartered, seeds removed, cut into chunks
1 small red onion, thinly sliced

1 garlic clove, finely chopped
120 ml (4 fl oz/$\frac{1}{2}$ cup) extra-virgin olive oil
2 tablespoons red wine vinegar
1 large handful flat-leaf (Italian) parsley leaves, coarsely chopped
Squeeze of lemon juice

YOGHURT-TAHINI DRESSING
300 g ($10\frac{1}{2}$ oz/$1\frac{1}{4}$ cups) Greek-style yoghurt
2 teaspoons tahini
1 teaspoon honey
1 garlic clove, finely chopped

Preheat the oven to 220°C (425°F). Place the lamb racks on a chopping board and season generously with the cumin and salt, using your fingers to rub the spice and the salt into the score marks. Heat a large frying pan over a high heat, add the oilve oil and sear the lamb for 2–3 minutes until golden brown all over, then transfer to a roasting tin. Roast until cooked to your liking (see note), covering the lamb with foil if it's getting too brown, then set aside to rest for 10–15 minutes.

Meanwhile, to make the quinoa salad, cook the quinoa in a saucepan of salted boiling water for about 10–12 minutes until tender, drain well, then spread on a tray to cool. Transfer to a bowl, add the tomatoes, cucumber, onion and garlic and season to taste.

Drizzle with the olive oil and vinegar, add the parsley and a squeeze of lemon and toss to combine.

To make the yoghurt-tahini dressing, combine the ingredients in a bowl, season to taste and whisk until smooth.

To serve, cut each rack of lamb into 3-cutlet sections, season with extra cumin and serve alongside the quinoa salad and yoghurt-tahini dressing.

NOTE As a guide, cook the lamb for 15–20 minutes for rare; 20–25 minutes for medium-rare; 30 minutes for medium and 35–40 minutes for well done.

MEATBALL SANDWICHES

Meatballs are an all-round family favourite in our house. Of course they're perfect with pasta, but I reckon they're even better stuffed into crusty ciabatta for a winner of a sandwich.

1 loaf of ciabatta
4 small handfuls wild rocket (arugula)
Finely grated parmesan cheese,
    to serve

TOMATO SAUCE
400 g (14 oz) tin of plum tomatoes
2 tablespoons olive oil
1 garlic clove, finely chopped
1 thyme sprig

PESTO
30 g (1 oz/1$\frac{1}{2}$ cups) basil, picked
100 ml (3$\frac{1}{2}$ fl oz) olive oil
1 tablespoon pine nuts
$\frac{1}{2}$ garlic clove, finely chopped
2 tablespoons finely grated
    parmesan cheese

MEATBALLS
2$\frac{1}{2}$ tablespoons olive oil
1 red onion, finely chopped
2 garlic cloves, finely chopped
500 g (1 lb 2 oz) beef mince
200 g (7 oz) pork mince
3 teaspoons finely chopped
    marjoram leaves
2 tablespoons finely chopped flat-leaf
    (Italian) parsley leaves
3 tablespoons finely grated
    parmesan cheese

To make the tomato sauce, combine the tomatoes, olive oil, garlic and thyme in a saucepan, season and bring to the boil over a medium–high heat. Reduce the heat to medium and simmer, stirring every now and then, for 15–20 minutes until thick and rich. Transfer to a blender, blend until smooth, then refrigerate until required.

To make the pesto, combine the basil, olive oil, pine nuts and garlic in a blender, season and blend for a minute or two until smooth. Transfer to a bowl, stir in the parmesan, check the seasoning and refrigerate until required.

To make the meatballs, heat a tablespoon of olive oil in a frying pan over a medium heat, add the onion and garlic, then sauté for a minute or two until tender and translucent and transfer to a bowl to cool. Add the beef and pork minces, herbs and parmesan, mix well with your hands to combine, then roll into 24 bite-sized balls. Heat the remaining oil in a large frying pan over medium heat, add the meatballs and fry for 3–4 minutes, turning occasionally to brown all over. Add the tomato sauce and simmer for 10–12 minutes, to cook the meatballs through.

Meanwhile, preheat the oven to 180°C (350°F). Place the bread in the oven for 5 minutes to warm through, then cut the loaf into four even pieces. Split each piece in half and spread a little pesto on both sides of each piece. Spoon in the meatballs and sauce, season to taste, add a handful of rocket to each roll and serve hot with the extra parmesan.

ROAST T-BONE with HERB BUTTER

I love a T-bone steak – it's hard to beat meat cooked on the bone for maximum flavour and succulence. If you can get your hands on dry-aged beef, which is becoming increasingly available at good butchers, be sure to snap it up. It's worth the extra cost. I prefer to cook a thicker steak to serve two. Make sure you take it out of the fridge about 40 minutes before cooking.

4 floury potatoes, such as Sebago, peeled and cut into chunks
100 ml (3½ fl oz) olive oil
2 x 500 g (1 lb 2 oz) T-bone steaks, at room temperature
1 handful wild rocket (arugula), to serve

HERB BUTTER
200 g (7 oz/¾ cup) butter, at room temperature
2 tablespoons finely chopped chives
2 tablespoons finely chopped tarragon leaves
1 tablespoon finely chopped flat-leaf (Italian) parsley leaves
1 tablespoon Dijon mustard
1 tablespoon Worcestershire sauce
3 anchovies, finely minced
1 garlic clove, finely chopped
½ teaspoon smoked paprika
Finely grated zest of ½ lemon

To make the herb butter, beat all the ingredients in a bowl to combine well and season to taste. If using straight away, keep at room temperature, or refrigerate until required – either in an airtight container or rolled the traditional way into a log. To do this, lay a piece of plastic wrap on your work bench and spoon the butter along one edge of the plastic wrap, about 10 cm (4 inches) in from the edges. Fold the plastic wrap over the butter to enclose and form a soft roll. Hold each end of the plastic wrap and twist, rolling on the bench to form a tight cylinder. Refrigerate for up to 5 days or freeze for up to 2 months.

Preheat the oven to 200°C (400°F). Combine the potatoes in a large saucepan with enough cold salted water to cover generously and bring to the boil over a high heat. Boil for 8–10 minutes until par-cooked, drain, then tip back into the pan and place over a low heat for a minute or so, shaking the pan to roughen the edges of the potatoes a little. Heat the oil in a roasting tin in the oven, then carefully add the potatoes to the tin, shaking to coat evenly in the oil. Season to taste and roast for 30–35 minutes until crisp and golden brown.

Meanwhile, heat a large ovenproof frying pan over a high heat. Season the steak generously, then rub the seasonings into the meat. Place the steak in the hot frying pan on the fat side and hold it there for a minute or so to render some of the fat from the beef. Once the fat browns, carefully place the steak on one side and fry for 1–2 minutes until a nice brown crust forms, then turn and brown the other side. Transfer to the oven to roast for 5–7 minutes for medium-rare. Set aside to rest for 10 minutes, then serve with the roast potatoes, herb butter and rocket.

ROAST DUCK SALAD with PINEAPPLE and CORIANDER

Buying a Chinese-style roasted duck is one of the best shortcuts you can take, especially if there's a Chinatown near you. It's so perfectly cooked, with such beautiful flavour and of course that glossy, lacquered skin. For a simple summer salad that's a meal in its own right, I pair it with slightly under-ripe pineapple to add a tart counterpoint to the richness of the duck. If you can't get roast duck, you could add seared sliced duck breast instead.

1 Chinese roast duck, at room
    temperature, meat coarsely
    shredded, skin coarsely torn
2 large handfuls watercress sprigs
1 large handful coriander (cilantro) sprigs
1 Lebanese (short) cucumber,
    coarsely chopped
$\frac{1}{2}$ under-ripe pineapple, peeled and
    coarsely chopped
60 g ($2\frac{1}{4}$ oz/$\frac{1}{2}$ cup) bean sprouts
3 spring onions (scallions), sliced

DRESSING

$2\frac{1}{2}$ tablespoons light soy sauce
$1\frac{1}{2}$ tablespoons rice vinegar
1 tablespoon hoisin sauce
1 tablespoon sesame oil
1 tablespoon vegetable oil
2 teaspoons finely grated fresh ginger
1 small garlic clove, finely chopped

Combine the duck meat and skin, watercress, coriander, cucumber, pineapple, bean sprouts and spring onion in a bowl and set aside.

Whisk the soy sauce, vinegar, hoisin sauce, oils, ginger and garlic in a bowl to combine, drizzle over the salad, toss lightly to combine and serve.

PIRI-PIRI CHICKEN with SMOKY TOMATO AIOLI

Piri-piri chicken has become part of the Australian food landscape – the smoky barbecue flavours are perfect for our style of eating in summer. I like to use chicken thighs on the bone, but you could use a whole butterflied chicken if you prefer. The traditional sauce to serve here is a garlic-chilli-tomato number, but I like to mix things up a bit with a smoky tomato aioli. A tomato salad such as the one on page 52 would work as a side, or try a simple rice pilaf. Lemon wedges to squeeze over are a must.

8 chicken thighs on the bone

MARINADE

6 garlic cloves
4 long red chillies, coarsely chopped
200 ml (7 fl oz) beer
200 ml (7 fl oz) dry white wine
Juice of 2 lemons, plus extra wedges
    to serve
2 tablespoons extra-virgin olive oil
4 fresh bay leaves
3 thyme sprigs, plus extra leaves to serve
3 teaspoons smoked paprika

SMOKY TOMATO AIOLI

100 g ($3\frac{1}{2}$ oz/$\frac{1}{2}$ cup) semi-dried tomatoes
2 garlic cloves
2 egg yolks
2 tablespoons red wine vinegar
$1\frac{1}{2}$ teaspoons smoked paprika
220 ml ($7\frac{1}{2}$ fl oz/scant 1 cup) olive oil
1 tablespoon lemon juice

To make the marinade, process the garlic and chillies in a food processor to a paste, then combine with the beer, wine, lemon juice, olive oil, bay leaves, thyme and paprika in a bowl and season. Slash the skin of the chicken thighs in several places, add to the marinade and mix well with your hands, rubbing the marinade into the cuts in the chicken. Cover with plastic wrap and refrigerate for a couple of hours to marinate.

While the chicken is marinating, make the smoky tomato aioli. Process the tomatoes, garlic and egg yolks in a food processor to combine and add the vinegar and paprika. Process to combine then, with the motor running, gradually drizzle in the oil, a little at a time, until thick and emulsified. Add the lemon juice and 1 tablespoon hot water, process to combine and season to taste.

Preheat a barbecue to a medium–high heat. Drain the chicken from the marinade and barbecue, skin-side down to begin with and turning occasionally, for 10–15 minutes until browned and cooked through. Set aside to rest for 5 minutes, then serve with the smoky tomato aioli.

FISH BURGERS

Any burger – be it a cheeseburger, beef burger or fish burger – is all about the pickles. They should be mouth-puckeringly tart, which is why I like to make my own, as store-bought pickles are often overly sweet.

Vegetable oil, for deep-frying
Seasoned plain (all-purpose) flour,
    for dusting
1 egg, lightly beaten
100 g (3½ oz/1⅔ cups) panko crumbs
4 x 120 g (4¼ oz) skinless firm white fish
    fillets, such as barramundi or cod
4 sesame brioche burger buns
¼ iceberg lettuce, shredded
2 tablespoons mayonnaise
Juice of ½ lemon

**QUICK CUCUMBER AND
ONION PICKLES**
400 ml (14 fl oz) rice vinegar
1½ tablespoons caster (superfine) sugar
½ teaspoon yellow mustard seeds
5 whole black peppercorns, crushed
1 clove
1 Lebanese (short) cucumber, thinly
    sliced into rounds
¼ red onion, thinly sliced into rings

To make the cucumber and onion pickles, stir the vinegar, sugar, spices and 125 ml (4 fl oz/½ cup) water in a saucepan over a medium–high heat until the sugar dissolves, then season with salt. Remove from the heat and stand to infuse for 10 minutes. Strain into a sterilised container and add the cucumber and onion, pressing to submerge. Cover and refrigerate for at least an hour and up to a couple of days to pickle – the longer you leave it, the better the flavour will be. Drain just before using.

Preheat the oil in a deep-fat fryer or large saucepan to 180°C (350°F). Set up three separate bowls – place the seasoned flour in one, the beaten egg in the next and the panko crumbs in the remaining bowl. Dust each piece of fish first in flour, then the

egg, shaking off excess in between. Dip into the crumbs, pressing the crumbs onto the fish to completely cover. Carefully deep-fry the fish in batches (be careful as hot oil will spit) for 3–4 minutes until golden brown and crisp. Drain on paper towels and season to taste.

While the fish is cooking, lightly toast the cut sides of the burger buns. Mix the lettuce, mayonnaise and lemon juice in a bowl to combine and season to taste.

To serve, pile a little lettuce mixture on each bun base, top with a piece of fish and then the pickles and serve hot.

GRILLED PRAWN SALAD with HOT and SOUR LEMONGRASS DRESSING

Thai food is so ubiquitous in Australia and its flavours have become a part of cooking for many of us. I'm no exception – I love the balance of hot, sour, salty and sweet that makes up any good Thai dish. They're the flavours that I've channelled here and I've added a good old Aussie twist by throwing barbecued prawns into the mix. You can buy fried shallots from Asian grocery shops, but if you can't get them, leave them out or fry your own.

200 g (7 oz) cherry tomatoes, halved
2 large handfuls coriander
(cilantro) leaves
2 large handfuls mint leaves
$\frac{1}{2}$ Lebanese (short) cucumber, peeled
into ribbons
3 kaffir lime leaves, thinly sliced
2 lemongrass stalks, white parts only,
thinly sliced
2 red Asian shallots, thinly sliced
2 small red chillies, thinly sliced
12 raw prawns (shrimp), peeled,
deveined, tails intact

2 teaspoons kecap manis
(sweet soy sauce)
Fried shallots, to serve

HOT AND SOUR LEMONGRASS DRESSING

100 ml ($3\frac{1}{2}$ fl oz) lime juice
70 ml ($2\frac{1}{4}$ fl oz) fish sauce
2 lemongrass stalks, white parts only,
thinly sliced
2 long green chillies, thinly sliced
1 garlic clove, thinly sliced
1 teaspoon caster (superfine) sugar

To make the hot and sour lemongrass dressing, stir the ingredients in a bowl to combine and set aside to infuse for about an hour.

Preheat a barbecue or chargrill pan to high. Combine the tomatoes, herbs, cucumber, lime leaves, lemongrass, red shallot and chilli in a large bowl and set aside. Brush the prawns with the kecap manis and barbecue for 1 minute or so on each side until just cooked through. Add to the salad mixture, drizzle with the dressing to taste and toss lightly to combine. Serve topped with fried shallots.

CHICKEN SCHNITZEL with a PARMESAN CRUST

A perfect 'schnitty' is the best dinner. Using Japanese panko crumbs guarantees a crisp crust, but if you can't get them, use rough sourdough breadcrumbs instead. Serve with mash or even the tangy green and white slaw on page 48.

4 small skinless chicken breast fillets
    (about 200 g/7 oz each)
100 g ($3\frac{1}{2}$ oz/$\frac{2}{3}$ cup) plain
    (all-purpose) flour
1 teaspoon paprika
2 eggs, lightly beaten
80 g ($2\frac{3}{4}$ oz/$1\frac{1}{3}$ cups) panko crumbs
50 g ($1\frac{3}{4}$ oz/$\frac{1}{2}$ cup) finely grated
    parmesan cheese

80 ml ($2\frac{1}{2}$ fl oz/$\frac{1}{3}$ cup) olive oil
100 g ($3\frac{1}{2}$ oz/$\frac{1}{3}$ cup) butter, diced
1 tablespoon sage leaves
1 garlic clove, thinly sliced
Finely grated zest of $\frac{1}{2}$ lemon
Juice of 1 lemon, plus extra wedges
    to serve

Preheat the oven to 180°C (350°F). Pound out each chicken breast between two pieces of baking paper with a mallet or rolling pin to about 5 mm ($\frac{1}{4}$ inch) thick.

Combine the flour and paprika in a bowl and season well. Place the beaten egg in a separate bowl. Place the panko crumbs and parmesan in a third bowl and season well.

Dust each piece of chicken in the flour mixture, then the egg and finally the panko crumb mixture, pressing the crumbs to coat the chicken. Place the chicken on a tray and set aside.

Heat a tablespoon of olive oil and knob of butter in a large frying pan over a medium–high heat until the butter foams. Add a schnitzel and fry for a minute or two until golden brown, turn and cook the remaining side, then transfer to a baking tray. Wipe out the pan and repeat with the remaining schnitzels, then bake for about 3–4 minutes until just cooked through.

Wipe out the frying pan again, add the remaining butter and cook for 2–3 minutes until nut brown. Remove from the heat, add the sage, garlic and lemon zest, season to taste, then squeeze in the lemon juice.

To serve, spoon the sage butter over the schnitzels and serve with extra lemon wedges to squeeze over.

PORK and FENNEL SAUSAGE PASTA with RED WINE

It's pretty hard to beat a great pasta for a quick weeknight meal and this is no exception. Using a good pork and fennel sausage as the base gives you a head start on the flavour front. I've used rigatoni here, but you could use any short pasta you have in the pantry. A short pasta is best, as it will hold the lovely chunky sauce well.

40 g (1½ oz/3 tablespoons) butter, diced
2 tablespoons olive oil
6 thick pork and fennel sausages
2 red onions, coarsely chopped
1 small fennel bulb, thinly sliced
2 tablespoons oregano, finely chopped,
    plus extra leaves to serve
2 garlic cloves, thinly sliced
1 teaspoon chilli flakes

1 teaspoon fennel seeds
150 ml (5 fl oz) red wine
400 g (14 oz) tin of chopped tomatoes
    or tin of cherry tomatoes
200 ml (7 fl oz) chicken stock
1 tablespoon balsamic vinegar
350 g (12 oz) dried rigatoni or other large
    tubular pasta
Finely grated parmesan cheese, to serve

Heat the butter and olive oil in a large saucepan over a medium–high heat until the butter foams. Squeeze the sausages out of their skins, discarding the skins, then break them into rough 1 cm (½ inch) pieces, add to the pan and fry, stirring occasionally, for about 2–3 minutes until starting to brown. Add the onion, fennel, oregano, garlic, chilli and fennel seeds and sauté, stirring occasionally, for 4–5 minutes until the onion and fennel are tender. Increase the heat to high, add the wine, mixing well, and simmer for a minute or two until the wine evaporates. Reduce the heat to low, add the tomatoes and chicken stock, season and simmer, stirring frequently, for 15–20 minutes until the sauce thickens. Stir in the vinegar and check the seasoning.

Meanwhile, bring a large saucepan of well-salted water to the boil. When the sauce is almost ready, add the rigatoni to the boiling water and give it a quick stir to stop the pasta sticking together, then boil until al dente – the exact time will depend on the pasta, but usually this will take 10–12 minutes. Drain, reserving a tablespoon or two of cooking water, then stir the pasta into the sausage mixture to coat well, adding some of the reserved cooking water to thin the sauce a little if necessary. Serve hot, scattered with oregano and grated parmesan.

ROAST CHICKEN MARYLANDS
with FENNEL and POTATO

The beauty of this recipe is that once the chopping is done, it's quite hands off. I've used chicken marylands, which is the whole leg of the chicken, but you can use a mix of chicken pieces on the bone. The rough herb dressing drizzled over at the end adds a burst of fresh flavour, but if you fancy taking a shortcut, you can skip this and give it a good squeeze of lemon instead. This is a mid-week go-to for me when I'm cooking at home, not least because there's minimal washing up!

4 chicken marylands, halved through the joint
1 garlic clove, finely chopped
1 teaspoon each finely chopped thyme and oregano leaves
80 ml ($2\frac{1}{2}$ fl oz/$\frac{1}{3}$ cup) olive oil
600 g (1 lb 5 oz) chat or other baby potatoes, thickly sliced
2 small fennel bulbs, cut into wedges, fronds reserved to serve
1 onion, cut into wedges
1 head of garlic, halved

$\frac{1}{2}$ lemon, thinly sliced, plus juice of remaining $\frac{1}{2}$
150 g ($5\frac{1}{2}$ oz) green beans, trimmed

ROUGH HERB DRESSING

2 tablespoons olive oil
2 teaspoons red wine vinegar
1 teaspoon lemon juice
1 tablespoon coarsely chopped thyme leaves
1 tablespoon coarsely chopped oregano leaves

Preheat the oven to 200°C (400°F). Combine the chicken pieces in a bowl with the chopped garlic, herbs and 1 tablespoon of the olive oil. Season and set aside.

Combine the potatoes, fennel wedges, onion, halved garlic and lemon slices in a bowl and season well. Drizzle with the remaining oil and toss to coat the vegetables evenly. Spread the mixture in two large roasting tins and roast, stirring occasionally, for 35–40 minutes until light golden brown and beginning to become tender. Arrange the chicken pieces on top, drizzle the chicken marinade over, squeeze over the lemon juice and roast for a further 35–40 minutes until the vegetables are tender and the chicken is browned and cooked through, adding the green beans to the pan for the last 10 minutes of cooking.

To make the rough herb dressing, mix all the ingredients in a bowl to combine and season to taste. Drizzle over the chicken and vegetables and serve hot.

THAI-STYLE FISH CURRY

A good curry is as much a part of many people's repertoire as meat and three veg, and it's all the better when made with a home-made curry paste. If I have time, I use a mortar and pestle to make a double batch of paste and then freeze half of it, so I'm a step ahead next time a curry craving hits. If I'm in a hurry, I'll make it in a food processor instead. Green curry is meant to be spicy and hot, but if you prefer a milder curry, adjust the chilli quantity to suit.

1 tablespoon coconut oil or vegetable oil
500 g (1 lb 2 oz) pumpkin (squash), peeled and cut into thin wedges
400 ml (14 fl oz) coconut cream
250 ml (9 fl oz/1 cup) chicken stock or water
3 long red chillies, split in half lengthways
4 kaffir lime leaves, crushed in your hand
80 ml (2½ fl oz/⅓ cup) fish sauce, plus extra to taste
1 tablespoon finely chopped palm sugar, plus extra to taste
4 x 200 g (7 oz) skinless firm white fish fillets, such as barramundi, blue-eye trevalla or cod
80 g (2¾ oz) snake (yard-long) beans, cut into rough 5 cm (2 inch) pieces
Juice of 1 lime, or to taste, plus extra wedges to serve
Thinly sliced small red chilli, to taste

Thai basil, coriander (cilantro) leaves and steamed jasmine rice, to serve

GREEN CURRY PASTE
6–8 green bird's eye chillies, or to taste
1½ tablespoons finely chopped galangal
3 lemongrass stalks, white parts only, finely chopped
3 kaffir lime leaves, finely chopped
1 teaspoon finely grated kaffir lime zest (optional)
3 coriander (cilantro) roots, soaked in water to remove grit, then drained and finely chopped
1 teaspoon finely chopped fresh turmeric or 1 teaspoon ground turmeric
3 red Asian shallots, coarsely chopped
6 garlic cloves, coarsely chopped
1 teaspoon shrimp paste

Make the curry paste by pounding the chillies in a mortar with a pinch of sea salt to form a paste. Add each of the remaining paste ingredients one at a time, pounding after each addition until a paste forms, then pound until homogenous.

Heat the oil over a medium–high heat, add the pumpkin and fry, turning occasionally, for 4–5 minutes until golden. Set aside.

Cook half of the coconut cream in a large saucepan over a high heat for 4–5 minutes until the coconut cream starts to separate and crack. Add the curry paste and stir for 6–8 minutes until it becomes aromatic and the raw taste has cooked out.

Add the remaining coconut cream and the stock, reserved pumpkin, chilli, lime leaves, fish sauce and sugar and simmer for about 8–10 minutes until well-flavoured and the pumpkin is tender.

Add the fish pieces in a single layer, then add the snake beans. Cover and simmer for a further 5–6 minutes until just cooked through. Add the lime juice and then taste to check the balance of flavours – it should taste spicy, sour, salty and sweet. Add a little extra sliced chilli, lime juice, fish sauce or palm sugar to your taste if you need to. Serve hot, scattered with Thai basil and coriander, with steamed rice.

TAGLIATELLE with PRAWNS, CHILLI and GARLIC

Hand-made pasta is one of my favourite things. I first learnt to make it as a young chef and it's been on the menu at many of my restaurants. I love making it at home with the kids when time permits – it's not a mid-week activity, of course! You'll need a pasta machine to make this.

6 vine-ripened tomatoes, cored and
　　bases scored
75 ml (2½ fl oz) extra-virgin olive oil
3 garlic cloves, finely chopped
1 long red chilli, seeds removed,
　　finely chopped
12 medium raw prawns (shrimp),
　　peeled and deveined
Juice of 1 lemon
10 basil leaves, torn, plus extra to serve

PASTA DOUGH
250 g (9 oz/1⅔ cups) 00 pasta flour,
　　plus extra for dusting
5 egg yolks
1 egg
2 teaspoons extra-virgin olive oil
½ teaspoon fine salt

To make the pasta dough, tip the flour into a mound on your work bench and make a well in the centre. Add the egg yolks and whole egg to the well with the olive oil and fine salt then, using your fingers, mix the egg mixture to combine. Start slowly, incorporating the flour from the edges of the well, mixing until it's all combined and a rough dough forms. Knead for 8–10 minutes until the pasta dough is smooth and elastic, then wrap in plastic wrap and rest at room temperature for at least 30 minutes.

Divide the dough into three pieces and flatten each slightly with a rolling pin. Working with one piece at a time, dust the pasta dough lightly with flour and pass through the widest setting of a pasta machine, folding and rolling as you go, reducing the settings notch by notch until you reach the second-lowest setting.

Cut the sheet of pasta into 30 cm (12 inch) lengths and pass through the tagliatelle cutter. Hang over a rod to dry or use the pasta fresh.

To make the sauce, blanch the tomatoes in a saucepan of boiling water for about 20 seconds until the skins split. Refresh in iced water to halt the cooking process, then drain and peel. Quarter the tomatoes, remove the seeds and discard, then cut the flesh into rough dice. Heat the olive oil in a large non-stick frying pan over a high heat, add the garlic and chilli and fry for a minute or so until fragrant, then add the prawns, season and cook, turning once, for a minute or two until just cooked through. Stir in the tomato and cook for about 2–3 minutes until just starting to break down.

Bring a large saucepan of well-salted water to the boil, add the pasta and cook for 2–3 minutes until al dente. Drain, reserving 4–5 tablespoons of the cooking water. Add the pasta and reserved pasta water to the sauce, squeeze in the lemon and add the basil, then toss to combine. Check the seasoning and serve hot, scattered with extra basil.

SPRING GREEN RISOTTO

Many people think of risotto as a time-consuming dish, but it's actually quite quick to cook. I get the rice on, then prep my veggies as it's cooking, leaning over to stir as needed.

1 tablespoon olive oil

60 g ($2\frac{1}{4}$ oz/$\frac{1}{4}$ cup) butter, diced

$\frac{1}{2}$ leek, white part only, diced

2 garlic cloves, finely chopped

200 g (7 oz/1 cup) arborio rice or vialone nano rice

100 ml ($3\frac{1}{2}$ fl oz) vermouth or dry white wine

1 litre (35 fl oz/4 cups) hot vegetable stock (see note)

150 g ($5\frac{1}{2}$ oz/1 cup) frozen peas, defrosted

100 g ($3\frac{1}{2}$ oz) sugar snap peas, trimmed and halved

1 bunch asparagus, trimmed and thinly sliced

1 zucchini (courgette), thinly sliced

Large handful baby English spinach

40 g ($1\frac{1}{2}$ oz/$\frac{1}{3}$ cup) finely grated parmesan cheese, plus extra to serve

Coarsely chopped thyme and mint leaves, to serve

Finely grated lemon zest, to serve

Heat the olive oil and a third of the butter in a large saucepan over a medium–high heat until the butter foams, reduce the heat to low–medium, add the leek and garlic and stir for 6–8 minutes until tender and translucent. Add the rice, stir for a minute or so to toast the rice and coat it in oil, then add the vermouth or wine and bring to the boil.

Add the hot stock, one ladleful at a time, stirring until each ladleful is absorbed before adding the next. Stir for 10–15 minutes until the rice is almost tender. Stir in the peas, sugar snap peas, asparagus and zucchini and cook for a minute or two until bright green and tender, then stir through the baby spinach to wilt. Stir in the parmesan and remaining butter to combine and serve hot, scattered with thyme, mint and lemon zest.

NOTE An excellent stock is key to a good risotto and for this vego version, I make my own to be sure of its quality. It's super-simple, you don't even need to peel the vegetables. Coarsely chop 2 carrots, 2 field mushrooms, 1 onion, 1 celery stalk and the green part of the leek and combine in a large saucepan. Add 1 halved head of garlic, 6 thyme sprigs and 1 teaspoon black peppercorns. Add 1.5 litres (52 fl oz/6 cups) cold water and a good pinch of sea salt, then bring to the boil. Reduce the heat to medium and simmer for about an hour for the flavour to develop, then strain through a fine sieve, discarding the solids. You can use this stock straight away or freeze it in containers for using later.

CHARGRILLED SPATCHCOCK with CHARRED CORN SALAD

Spatchcock (also called poussin) are young chickens that weigh in at about 500 g/1 lb 2 oz each. They're becoming more readily available from good butchers and specialist poultry shops, but you may need to plan ahead a little and order in advance. They're the perfect size to serve one person – no more arguments about who gets the breast or thigh, as with this little bird you get some of everything. They're great cooked on the barbie as the skin gets nice and crisp and cooking the meat on the bone prevents it from drying out. Win-win!

4 spatchcock (about 500 g/1 lb 2 oz each), butterflied
60 ml (2 fl oz/¼ cup) olive oil, plus extra for drizzling
1 tablespoon lime juice, plus extra lime wedges to serve
1 garlic clove, finely chopped
1 teaspoon each sweet paprika, smoked paprika and ground cumin
4 corn cobs, husks and silk removed

6 spring onions (scallions), trimmed
1 avocado, cut into wedges
1 baby gem lettuce, cut into thin wedges

SOUR CREAM VINAIGRETTE
2 tablespoons extra-virgin olive oil
1½ tablespoons sour cream
1 tablespoon white wine vinegar
1 tablespoon lime juice
1 garlic clove, finely chopped

Preheat a chargrill pan or barbecue to a medium–high heat. Combine the spatchcock in a bowl with the olive oil, lime juice, garlic and spices, season and massage the marinade into the spatchcock. Set aside to marinate for about 30 minutes.

To make the vinaigrette, whisk the ingredients in a bowl with 1 tablespoon water until smooth and combined. Season to taste and set aside for the flavours to develop.

Drizzle the corn and the spring onions with a little olive oil and chargrill or barbecue, turning occasionally, until slightly charred and tender – the corn cobs will take 6–8 minutes, the spring onion will only take a minute or so. When the corn is cool enough

to handle, cut the kernels from the cob, keeping in clusters, then transfer to a bowl. Coarsely chop the spring onion and add to the corn.

Drain the spatchcock from the marinade and chargrill, skin-side down, for 4–5 minutes until browned, then turn and cook the remaining side for 4–5 minutes until just cooked through. Set aside to rest for 5 minutes.

Add the avocado and lettuce to the corn mixture, drizzle with the dressing to taste and toss lightly to combine. Serve alongside the spatchcock with lime wedges, drizzled with any of the juices that collect after resting.

SALT-BAKED SNAPPER

Baking fish in a salt crust creates maximum flavour and incredible moistness and I love the theatre of cracking into the salt crust at the table to reveal the beautiful fish inside. I keep the sides to this simple – steamed baby beans are ideal or try the butter lettuce with peas and preserved lemon on page 31 (although I'd skip the goat's cheese).

1 snapper or other whole fish
   (about 1.5 kg/3 lb 5 oz)
1 lemon, cut into 6 slices, plus extra
   wedges to serve
1 small fennel bulb, trimmed, cut into
   6 slices, fronds reserved
3 fresh bay leaves

2 kg (4 lb 8 oz) rock salt
1 tablespoon fennel seeds,
   coarsely crushed
1 tablespoon coriander seeds,
   coarsely crushed
Extra-virgin olive oil, for drizzling

Preheat the oven to 200°C (400°F). Stuff the cavity of the snapper with the slices of lemon and fennel, as well as the bay leaves.

Combine the salt, crushed spices and 250 ml (9 fl oz/1 cup) water in a bowl and mix together well. Line a baking tray with baking paper and spread a third of the salt crust mixture on the tray. Place the snapper on top, and then mound the remaining salt mixture evenly over the fish to completely enclose. Bake for 30 minutes, then stand for 5 minutes.

To serve, crack the salt crust and brush away from the fish. Peel away the skin to reveal the moist flesh, carefully remove the flesh from the bone and serve drizzled with olive oil with the lemon wedges squeezed over.

RED LENTIL DHAL

Australian cooking has transformed in a relatively short space of time
from quite bland to an increased use of fragrant exotic spices. There are
some great Aussie-grown red lentils on the market now too, which have a
little more texture than regular red lentils, which break down quite quickly.
Regardless of which lentils you use, this dhal will be a knock-out – it's so
full of flavour.

400 ml (14 fl oz) coconut milk
230 g (8 oz) red lentils, rinsed
  and drained
1 onion, finely chopped
40 g (1½ oz) fresh ginger, finely grated
3 garlic cloves, crushed
2 teaspoons ground turmeric
2 teaspoons Madras curry powder
2 cinnamon sticks
12 fresh curry leaves, plus extra to serve
2 long green chillies, thinly sliced
Juice of 2 limes, or to taste,
  plus lime wedges to serve

200 ml (7 fl oz) coconut cream,
  plus extra to serve
Coarsely chopped coriander (cilantro)
  leaves, to serve

TADKA
2 tablespoons ghee or coconut oil
1 onion, thinly sliced
3 garlic cloves, finely chopped
1 teaspoon brown mustard seeds
1 teaspoon chilli flakes
Pinch of garam masala

Combine the coconut milk, lentils, onion, ginger, garlic, turmeric, curry powder, cinnamon, curry leaves and chilli in a saucepan with 750 ml (26 fl oz/3 cups) water. Bring to the boil, reduce the heat to medium and simmer, covered, for 10–15 minutes, stirring occasionally, until the lentils are tender and broken down.

Squeeze in the lime juice, add the coconut cream and season the lentils generously.

For the tadka, melt the ghee or coconut oil in a saucepan over a medium heat, add the onion, garlic, mustard seeds, chilli and garam masala and fry for 1–2 minutes until fragrant, and then stir half into the lentil mixture.

Ladle the dhal into bowls, drizzle with extra coconut cream, spoon over the remaining tadka and serve hot, scattered with chopped coriander, curry leaves and lime wedges.

GRILLED BARRAMUNDI CUTLETS with OREGANO, TOMATO and BLACK OLIVES

So often we cook fillets of fish, but just like meat, fish is excellent cooked on the bone, whether it's as a whole fish (which I love) or as cutlets, as I've done here. You can ask your fishmonger to prepare the cutlets. I've kept it super-simple with this tomato and black olive sauce – all you need is a vinaigrette-dressed potato salad or roast baby potatoes to make it a meal.

2 tablespoons dried oregano
2 garlic cloves, finely chopped
Finely grated zest and juice of 2 lemons, plus extra wedges to serve
200 ml (7 fl oz) olive oil

4 vine-ripened tomatoes, cored and bases scored
4 tablespoons black olives, pitted and finely chopped
6 x 200 g (7 oz) barramundi cutlets or other fish cutlets

Pound the oregano, garlic and lemon zest in a mortar and pestle with a good amount of seasoning to a coarse paste. Stir in the olive oil and lemon juice.

Place the fish in a single layer in a glass or ceramic dish, pour over half the oregano dressing, turn to coat, cover and refrigerate for an hour to marinate.

While the barramundi is marinating, bring a saucepan of water to the boil over a high heat, add the tomatoes and blanch for 30 seconds until the skins split, then transfer to iced water to refresh. Drain again, then peel the tomatoes, scoop out the seeds and dice the flesh. Add to the remaining dressing along with the olives and set aside.

Preheat a barbecue or chargrill pan to a high heat. Drain the barramundi from the marinade and barbecue or chargrill, turning once, for 8–10 minutes until just cooked through. Serve the fish hot with the tomato dressing spooned on top and lemon wedges to squeeze over.

BARNSLEY CHOPS with MASH
and MINTY PEAS

I love all cuts of lamb (and beef and pork, for that matter), but a favourite is the Barnsley chop. A Barnsley chop is essentially a double loin chop, cut right across the saddle, so you get two sections of tenderloin and two of the eye fillet, all attached to the T-bone. It's a generous cut, so it's generally one per person. You'll probably need to give your butcher a day or so notice to get them to prepare them for you.

4 Barnsley lamb chops,
    at room temperature
60 g (2¼ oz/¼ cup) butter, diced
1 tablespoon olive oil
3 anchovies, coarsely chopped
1 garlic clove, finely chopped
200 ml (7 fl oz) veal stock
350 g (12 oz/2½ cups) frozen
    peas, defrosted
Good handful torn mint leaves
Squeeze of lemon juice

GARLIC MASH
1 kg (2 lb 4 oz) floury potatoes,
    such as Sebago, peeled and cut
    into even chunks
125 ml (4 fl oz/½ cup) single
    (pure/pouring) cream
60 g (2¼ oz/¼ cup) butter, diced
1 garlic clove, finely chopped

To make the garlic mash, combine the potatoes and enough cold salted water to cover generously in a large saucepan. Bring to the boil over a high heat and cook for 10–12 minutes until the potatoes are tender when pierced with the tip of a paring knife.

Meanwhile, bring the cream, butter and garlic to a simmer in a separate saucepan and set aside. When the potatoes are cooked, drain well, return to the pan and mash with a fork or masher. Add the cream mixture, season generously and mix until smooth. Keep warm.

Season the chops generously. Heat a large frying pan over a medium heat with the butter and olive oil. Place the chops in the pan and cook, turning over every minute, for 6–8 minutes, then transfer to a plate to rest.

Add the anchovies and garlic to the pan and fry for a minute or so until fragrant, then add the stock and bring to the boil. Toss in the peas, season and simmer for a minute until bright green and just tender. Stir in the mint and lemon juice to taste and serve spooned over the chops and mash.

BEST BEEF BURGERS

There are plenty of opinions when it comes to what makes the best burgers. For me, it's keeping the patty itself all about the meat – no onion, breadcrumbs or egg, just beef with a decent fat ratio and plenty of salt and pepper. Avoid lean beef at all costs or you'll end up with the driest burger. Non-negotiables are fried onions, sliced tomato and shredded lettuce. The rest is up to you. I like to go old-school Aussie milk bar and add beetroot relish and, of course, some sauce (I'm not going to go into the tomato sauce vs barbecue sauce debate!). Or head down the cheeseburger route and go for pickles and mayo. Fries optional.

500 g (1 lb 2 oz) beef mince
3 tablespoons olive oil
1 onion, thinly sliced into rings
4 soft burger buns, halved and
    cut sides toasted
Tomato sauce, barbecue sauce
    and/or mayonnaise
2 tomatoes, thickly sliced
$\frac{1}{4}$ iceberg lettuce or $\frac{1}{2}$ baby cos lettuce,
    coarsely shredded

BEETROOT RELISH

2 tablespoons olive oil
$\frac{1}{2}$ red onion, finely diced
1 garlic clove, finely chopped
250 g (9 oz) beetroot (beets) (about
    2 medium beetroot), peeled and cut
    into julienne or coarsely grated
3 thyme sprigs
60 ml (2 fl oz/$\frac{1}{4}$ cup) red wine vinegar
$1\frac{1}{2}$ tablespoons brown sugar

To make the beetroot relish, heat the olive oil in a saucepan over a medium–high heat, add the onion and garlic and sauté, stirring occasionally, for a minute or two until the onion is tender and translucent. Stir in the beetroot and thyme and cook, stirring occasionally, for 2–3 minutes until beginning to soften, then stir in the vinegar, sugar and 2 tablespoons water, season and simmer for 7–8 minutes until the beetroot is just tender and the liquid is evaporated. Cool, then refrigerate for up to 2 weeks in a sterilised jar.

Divide the mince into four and form each into a loose patty just a little bit bigger than your burger buns. Place on a tray and refrigerate for about 15 minutes.

Heat half the olive oil in a frying pan over a medium–high heat, add the onion and fry, stirring occasionally, for 7–8 minutes until browned and tender. Season to taste and transfer to a bowl.

Wipe out the pan with paper towels and add the remaining oil. Season both sides of the patties generously and fry, turning once, for just 1–2 minutes until browned and not quite cooked through.

Spread the bun bases with sauce and/or mayonnaise, then top each with a burger patty, onion, tomato, a little beetroot relish, lettuce and more mayo, if desired, then sandwich with the burger bun tops and serve.

LOBSTER with GARLIC BUTTER

Lobster is an absolute luxury. At ARIA Sydney a popular dish is our lobster French toast, featuring Champagne lobster and caviar. If I'm cooking lobster at home, it's usually for a celebration – a birthday, an anniversary, or as part of a Christmas feast. My approach at home is simpler than at the restaurant though – it's all about fresh flavours that highlight the beautiful sweetness of this amazing crustacean.

800 g (1 lb 12 oz) live lobster
6 garlic cloves, unpeeled
200 g (7 oz/$\frac{3}{4}$ cup) butter, diced
$2\frac{1}{2}$ tablespoons white wine vinegar
1 French shallot, thinly sliced
1 thyme sprig

1 fresh bay leaf
1 egg yolk
Juice of $\frac{1}{2}$ lemon
2 teaspoons finely chopped
   tarragon leaves

To prepare the lobster, place into a freezer for at least an hour to render it insensible – if the tail can be easily moved without resistance, the lobster is insensible. Remove from the freezer, cut through the centreline of the head with a large sharp knife, then cook in a large saucepan of well-salted boiling water for 1 minute. Transfer to a bowl of iced water to stop the cooking process, then once the lobster is chilled, drain and refrigerate until required.

Preheat the oven to 180°C (350°F). Wrap the garlic cloves in foil, place them on a baking tray and roast for about 25–30 minutes or until the garlic is tender, then set aside to cool. Meanwhile, soften half the butter at room temperature. Peel the roast garlic, mash to a fine paste, then stir into the softened butter and season.

Melt the remaining butter in a small saucepan over a low heat and keep warm.

Combine the vinegar, shallot, thyme and bay leaf in a small saucepan and simmer over a medium–high heat for 1–2 minutes until the vinegar reduces by half. Strain through a sieve into a

bowl, add the egg yolk and 1 tablespoon cold water, season and whisk to combine. Whisk continuously over a saucepan of gently simmering water for 2–3 minutes until fluffy, then remove from the heat. Whisking continuously, gradually drizzle a little of the melted butter into the bowl, whisking to incorporate before adding more, until all the butter is incorporated and emulsified. Whisk in the lemon juice and tarragon, check the seasoning and set aside in a warm place.

Preheat a grill (broiler) to its hottest setting. Using a large knife, cut the lobster in half from the head to the tail through the shell. Remove the brown contents from the head and the intestinal tract that runs down to its tail. Carefully pull the lobster meat from the tail and the head then cut the meat into eight pieces.

Spread half of the garlic butter along the inside of the lobster shells, then return the meat to each of the shells. Spread a little more garlic butter over the lobster meat, then season. Grill (broil) for 8–10 minutes until the butter is bubbling and the lobster flesh becomes opaque, then serve with tarragon sauce spooned over.

ROCKMELON and GINGER GRANITA

A granita is one of the simplest icy treats you can make. There's no need for an ice-cream machine – it's a simple case of popping the mixture into the freezer and scraping every now and again with a fork as the ice crystals form. You can make a granita with almost any fruit. The key is to get the right balance of sweetness, as if there's too much sugar in the mix, it won't freeze properly. For an adults-only treat, you could also add a splash of gin or vodka to this recipe, but again, don't add too much or it won't freeze.

165 g (5¾ oz/¾ cup) caster
(superfine) sugar
1 medium rockmelon (cantaloupe),
peeled, seeds scooped out,
flesh coarsely chopped

375 ml (13 fl oz/1½ cups) good-quality
ginger beer
50 g (1¾ oz) fresh ginger, peeled and
coarsely grated
Juice of 2 limes, or to taste

Stir the sugar and 80 ml (2½ fl oz/⅓ cup) water in a small saucepan over a medium–high heat until the sugar dissolves. Bring to the boil for 1 minute, then remove from the heat and allow to cool to room temperature.

Blend the rockmelon and half the ginger beer in a blender for a minute or two to a fine purée, then strain through a sieve. Stir in the remaining ginger beer and add the sugar syrup to taste. Squeeze the juice of the grated ginger into the rockmelon mixture through a fine sieve, discarding the solids, then stir in the lime juice, to taste.

Pour into a metal tray or cake tin and freeze overnight, scraping with a fork every so often to form ice crystals. Cover and freeze until required and scrape again with a fork before serving so the ice crystals are nice and fluffy. The granita will freeze well for a couple of weeks. Serve in chilled glasses or bowls.

RICE PUDDING with STRAWBERRIES and PISTACHIOS

Rice pudding is one of those old-school comfort foods, most often cooked and eaten in winter. There's no reason you can't enjoy it in summer too, although in this case I'd serve it chilled, scattered with the season's best strawberries.

1 tablespoon unsalted butter, diced
120 g ($4\frac{1}{4}$ oz) short-grain rice,
   such as arborio
560 ml ($19\frac{1}{4}$ fl oz/$2\frac{1}{4}$ cups) single
   (pure/pouring) cream
560 ml ($19\frac{1}{4}$ fl oz/$2\frac{1}{4}$ cups) milk
1 vanilla bean, split and seeds scraped
110 g ($3\frac{3}{4}$ oz/$\frac{1}{2}$ cup) caster
   (superfine) sugar

2 egg yolks
250 g (9 oz) strawberries, hulled,
   cut into wedges
1 teaspoon icing (confectioners') sugar
Few drops of lemon juice
Coarsely chopped pistachios and
   mint leaves, to serve

Preheat the oven to 110°C (225°F). Melt the butter in an ovenproof saucepan over a low heat, add the rice and stir for a minute or two to coat the rice in the butter and lightly toast. Add the cream, milk, vanilla bean and seeds and 80 g ($2\frac{3}{4}$ oz/$\frac{1}{3}$ cup) of the sugar and simmer, stirring frequently, for 10–15 minutes.

Cover with a tight-fitting lid and bake for 50 minutes–1 hour, stirring the rice mixture every 15 minutes or so to prevent the rice from sticking to the bottom of the saucepan.

Whisk the yolks and remaining sugar in a bowl for 1–2 minutes until light and fluffy, then stir into the rice mixture. Return to the stove top and stir continuously over a medium–high heat for a minute or two to thicken slightly. Discard the vanilla bean and refrigerate to chill.

To serve, combine the strawberries, icing sugar and lemon juice in a bowl and toss to coat, then spoon the strawberries and their juices over the rice pudding. Serve scattered with pistachios and mint leaves.

MANGO POPS
(with a hit of cayenne salt)

When mangoes are in season, I can't get enough of them. I often buy them by the trayful, so apart from eating them without ceremony standing over the kitchen sink to catch the juices, I'll often turn them into popsicles like these. The cayenne salt adds a grown-up kick and unexpected flavour, which is extremely more-ish.

160 g (5½ oz/⅔ cup) caster
   (superfine) sugar
3 ripe mangoes
80 ml (2½ fl oz/⅓ cup) freshly squeezed
   lime juice, plus lime wedges to serve

CAYENNE SALT
2 teaspoons sea salt flakes
2 teaspoons caster (superfine) sugar
½ teaspoon cayenne pepper, or to taste

Combine the sugar and 170 ml (5½ fl oz/⅔ cup) water in a saucepan over a medium–high heat, stir to dissolve, then bring to the boil. Remove from the heat and set aside to cool.

Cut the cheeks off the mangoes and use a large metal spoon to scoop the flesh out of the cheeks. Cut off as much flesh as you can from around the seeds too. Coarsely chop the flesh and process the mango and lime juice in a food processor until smooth, then add sugar syrup to taste (you may not need it all, depending on the sweetness of the mango) and process to combine.

Pour into popsicle moulds, freeze for about an hour until half-frozen, then insert sticks and freeze for about 2 hours until frozen through. The pops will keep at this stage for up to a month. To un-mould, dip the moulds in hot water, wiggle the pops to loosen, then remove from the moulds and place on a tray lined with baking paper, returning to the freezer until frozen firm again. Store the pops in a single layer in an airtight container for up to 3 weeks.

For the cayenne salt, combine all the ingredients in a bowl. Dip the pops in cayenne salt to serve and squeeze over extra lime wedges, if you like.

COCONUT and LIME MARSHMALLOWS

Marshmallows have a timeless appeal – they remind me of school fetes
and country shows. These featherlight home-made ones are no exception
and the combination of tangy lime and toasty coconut make them
pretty much irresistible.

325 g (11½ oz/1½ cups) caster
   (superfine) sugar
50 g (1¾ oz) liquid glucose
4 egg whites

12 titanium strength gelatine leaves,
   softened in cold water for 5 minutes
Finely grated zest of 2 limes
250 g (9 oz/2¾ cups) desiccated
   (shredded) coconut

Line a 20 x 30 cm (8 x 12 inch) cake tin with baking paper. Stir the sugar, glucose and 200 ml (7 fl oz/¾ cup) water in a small saucepan over a medium–high heat until the sugar dissolves. Place a sugar thermometer into the syrup and boil without stirring for 12–15 minutes until the syrup reaches 125°C (255°F).

Meanwhile, whisk the egg whites and a pinch of salt in an electric mixer for 2–3 minutes until soft peaks form then, with the mixer on medium speed, gradually add the hot syrup. Once all the syrup is added, squeeze the excess water from the gelatine, add to the egg white mixture and whisk for 8–10 minutes until thick and fluffy and doubled in size. Stir in the lime zest, spoon the marshmallow into the tray, smooth the top with a wet palette knife and refrigerate for 3–4 hours to set.

Preheat the oven to 180°C (350°F). Spread the desiccated coconut on a baking tray and bake in the oven, stirring occasionally, for 4–5 minutes until golden brown, then set aside to cool.

Scatter some of the coconut onto a chopping board and tip the marshmallow onto the coconut. Carefully remove the baking paper and scatter more coconut on top. Using a large hot and wet knife, cut the marshmallow into cubes, then place in a bowl with the remaining coconut and toss to coat. Store in an airtight container in the refrigerator for up to 5 days.

SOUR CHERRY, PISTACHIO and CHOCOLATE PARFAIT

A parfait is a great way to enjoy ice cream at home without the need for an ice-cream machine. This one is studded with dried sour cherries, dark chocolate and pistachios, but you could use any combination of dried fruits and nuts that take your fancy. Serve in scoops or freeze in a loaf tin and serve as slices.

9 egg yolks
250 g (9 oz/generous 1 cup) caster (superfine) sugar
1 vanilla bean, split and seeds scraped
600 ml (21 fl oz) thickened (whipping) cream
250 g (9 oz/1 cup) crème fraîche
80 g (2¾ oz/½ cup) roasted pistachios, coarsely chopped, plus extra to serve
100 g (3½ oz/⅔ cup) dried sour cherries, coarsely chopped

80 g (2¾ oz) dark chocolate, coarsely chopped, plus extra coarsely grated to serve
Raspberries, to serve

RASPBERRY COULIS
250 g (9 oz) raspberries
2 tablespoons icing (confectioners') sugar

Whisk the egg yolks, sugar and vanilla seeds in a heatproof bowl to combine, then place over a saucepan of simmering water (make sure the water doesn't touch the base of the bowl) and whisk for 6–8 minutes until very pale and the mixture doubles in volume. Transfer to an electric mixer and whisk for 8–10 minutes until cool.

Whisk the thickened cream and crème fraîche until stiff peaks form, then fold into the cooled egg mixture, along with the pistachios, dried cherries and chocolate. Transfer to a container, cover and freeze overnight (and for up to 2 weeks).

To make the raspberry coulis, blend the raspberries and icing sugar in a food processor to a smooth purée, then pass through a fine sieve to remove the seeds and refrigerate until required.

Serve scoops of parfait in chilled bowls with raspberry coulis, scattered with extra pistachios, chocolate and raspberries.

PASSIONFRUIT CHEESECAKE

We take passionfruit for granted in Australia. For many of us, they're the flavour and fragrance of childhood and we use them with abandon. I didn't realise what a luxury this was until I went overseas, where passionfruit are often hard to get. This cheesecake is a celebration of them at their best and is best made the day before you want to eat it.

PASTRY
140 g (5 oz/generous $\frac{1}{2}$ cup) unsalted
    butter, softened
140 g (5 oz/scant 1 cup) plain
    (all-purpose) flour
140 g (5 oz/scant $\frac{2}{3}$ cup) caster
    (superfine) sugar
140 g (5 oz/1$\frac{1}{3}$ cups) almond meal
1 teaspoon salt

MASCARPONE FILLING
400 g (14 oz/1$\frac{3}{4}$ cups) caster
    (superfine) sugar
300 g (10$\frac{1}{2}$ oz/1$\frac{1}{4}$ cups) mascarpone
    cheese

150 g (5$\frac{1}{2}$ oz/$\frac{2}{3}$ cup) cream cheese, diced,
    at room temperature
1 vanilla bean, split and seeds scraped
2 eggs
8 egg yolks

PASSIONFRUIT JELLY
Pulp of 6 passionfruit, plus extra to serve
75 ml (2$\frac{1}{2}$ fl oz/$\frac{1}{4}$ cup) orange juice
2 teaspoons caster (superfine) sugar
1$\frac{1}{2}$ titanium strength gelatine leaves,
    softened in cold water for 5 minutes

Preheat the oven to 160°C (315°F) and line a 4 cm (1$\frac{1}{2}$ inch) deep, 25 x 32 cm (10 x 13 inch) baking tray with baking paper. To make the pastry, process the butter, flour, sugar, almond meal and salt in a food processor for 1–2 minutes until combined. Press evenly into the base of the prepared tray and bake for 25–35 minutes until the pastry is dark golden brown, then set aside to cool for 20 minutes.

Reduce the oven temperature to 110°C (225°F). To make the mascarpone filling, process the sugar, mascarpone, cream cheese and vanilla seeds in a food processor to combine, add the eggs and yolks and process until smooth, being careful not to over-blend as the mixture will split. Pour over the pastry base and bake for 25–30 minutes, turning the tray partway through cooking to help it cook evenly, until the filling is set with a slight wobble in the middle. Cool at room temperature for 30 minutes, then refrigerate to chill completely - overnight is best.

To make the passionfruit jelly, process the passionfruit pulp (reserving 2 teaspoons of the pulp) in a food processor to crack the seeds and release the juices, then strain through a fine sieve to yield 75 ml (2$\frac{1}{2}$ fl oz/$\frac{1}{4}$ cup) juice. Transfer to a small saucepan, add the orange juice, sugar, 1 tablespoon water and reserved pulp and warm over a low heat, stirring until the sugar dissolves and the liquid reaches 80°C (175°F). Squeeze the excess water from the gelatine, add to the passionfruit mixture and stir to dissolve. Cool to room temperature, then pour gently over the cheesecake, ensuring the seeds are evenly distributed.

Return the cheesecake to the refrigerator for an hour to set. To serve, remove from the baking tray, cut into portions and garnish with extra passionfruit pulp.

PAVLOVA with RASPBERRIES

The debate about the origins of pavlova shows no signs of abating (yes, I'm looking at you, New Zealanders!), so I'm going to stake my claim for Australia. Older eggs are the best for pavlovas as their runnier whites give more volume, so make sure you keep any egg whites left over from making mayonnaise or custard and store them in the freezer for when you want to make a pav. Defrost them first, of course, and if you think far enough ahead, leave them at room temperature overnight for an even better result.

5 egg whites
½ vanilla bean, split and seeds scraped
250 g (9 oz/generous 1 cup) caster (superfine) sugar
2 teaspoons cornflour (cornstarch)
1 teaspoon white wine vinegar

500 ml (17 fl oz/2 cups) thickened (whipping) cream
50 g (1¾ oz/scant ½ cup) icing (confectioners') sugar, sieved, plus extra to serve
375 g (13 oz) raspberries

Preheat the oven to 120°C (235°F). Trace a 20 cm (8 inch) circle on a piece of baking paper with a pencil, using a cake tin as a template, then place the paper pencil-side down on a lightly oiled baking tray.

Whisk the egg whites, vanilla seeds and a pinch of salt in the clean bowl of an electric mixer for 2–3 minutes until soft peaks form, then gradually add the caster sugar, whisking until everything is well combined.

Sieve in the cornflour, add the vinegar and whisk for 4–5 minutes until the egg whites are stiff and glossy peaks form.

Spoon the meringue into a high 20 cm (8 inch) mound, using the circle as a guide, then slightly flatten the top and bake for 1½–2 hours until crisp but not coloured. Turn off the oven and cool the pav completely in the oven (this will take 3–4 hours).

To make the filling, whisk the cream and icing sugar until soft peaks form, then add a third of the raspberries to the cream and whisk until the cream thickens and holds its shape.

To serve, place the pavlova on a serving plate and pile the raspberry cream on top. Scatter with the remaining raspberries, dust with extra icing sugar and serve.

TRIPLE-CHOCOLATE TARTLETS

There's a bit of work in these little guys, but when you bite into one, all the hard work is worth it! If you don't have individual tart tins, you can make a large tart instead – a 23 cm (9 inch) diameter tart tin will do the trick.

160 ml (5¼ fl oz/⅔ cup) single (pure/pouring) cream
2 tablespoons whisky
200 g (7 oz) dark chocolate (about 65–70 % cocoa solids), coarsely chopped
Sea salt flakes, to serve

CHOCOLATE PASTRY

200 g (7 oz/1⅓ cups) plain (all-purpose) flour
60 g (2¼ oz/½ cup) icing (confectioners') sugar, sifted

30 g (1 oz/¼ cup) Dutch-process cocoa
120 g (4¼ oz/½ cup) cold butter, diced
2 egg yolks

CHOCOLATE-PRALINE FILLING

80 g (2¾ oz/½ cup) hazelnuts
90 g (3¼ oz/scant ½ cup) caster (superfine) sugar
200 ml (7 fl oz) single (pure/pouring) cream
250 g (9 oz) couverture milk chocolate, finely chopped

To make the chocolate pastry, process the flour, icing sugar, cocoa and a good pinch of sea salt in a food processor to combine. Add the butter, process until the mixture resembles fine crumbs, then add the yolks and 1 tablespoon iced water and process to combine. Turn onto a lightly floured work surface and bring the pastry together with the heel of your hand, then wrap in plastic wrap and refrigerate for 1 hour to rest.

Divide the pastry into six and roll out each piece on a lightly floured surface to 3 mm (⅛ inch) thick. Line six 10 cm (4 inch) diameter individual tart tins, letting the excess pastry overhang the sides, then refrigerate to rest for 1 hour. Preheat the oven to 180°C (350°F). Trim the excess pastry, then line the tartlet cases with baking paper and fill with raw rice or baking weights and blind-bake for 10–12 minutes until the edges of the pastry are dry to touch. Remove the baking paper and weights and bake for a further 10–12 minutes until the bases are dry and crisp, then set aside.

For the chocolate-praline filling, spread the hazelnuts on a baking tray and roast for 5–6 minutes until the skins darken. Tip into a clean tea towel, rub off the skins, and then spread

the nuts on a lightly oiled baking tray. Stir the sugar and 60 ml (2 fl oz/¼ cup) water in a small saucepan over a medium–high heat until the sugar dissolves. Bring to the boil, brush down the sides of the pan with a wet pastry brush to remove the sugar crystals and cook for 3–4 minutes, swirling the pan occasionally until dark caramel in colour. Pour over the hazelnuts; stand until cool and set, and then break into rough pieces. Process in a food processor until the praline is finely ground and set aside. Bring the cream to a simmer in a small saucepan over a medium heat, add the milk chocolate and stir until smooth. Remove from the heat, stir in two-thirds of the praline mixture, reserving the remaining praline in an airtight container to serve, and pour into the tartlet cases, filling to about 4 mm (¼ inch) below the rim of the pastry cases. Refrigerate for an hour or so until firm.

Bring the cream and whisky to a simmer in a small saucepan over a medium–high heat, add the dark chocolate, remove from the heat and stand for 5 minutes, stirring until smooth. Pour over the praline filling and refrigerate for about 1 hour or until set (the tarts will keep refrigerated for up to 2 days). Serve scattered with the extra praline and a little sea salt.

PART TWO

COUNTRY

C O U N T R Y

When I think of food at the farm, the first thing that comes to mind are my nan, Valda's, date scones. To me, these melt-in-the-mouth, fruit-laden scones represent all that's great about country cooking. There are no airs and graces and, for Nan, there was no messing around with weights and measures – it was all done by eye. Without fail, those scones would be spot on, every time. Although Nan's no longer with us, I'll still make a batch of her scones whenever I'm down at the farm.

Time is on my side when I'm there – it's about slowing down and really enjoying the process of cooking. It's cold-weather country (there's snow most years) so that influences the way I cook there too. Low and slow is the order of the day, whether it's a rich braise or a hearty soup. Breakfasts are long and lazy, lunches stretch into dinners and friends often drop by, so many of these dishes need to feed a crowd.

Of course, there's plenty of lamb (I'd be crazy not to take advantage of the lamb we have on the farm) and it's pretty hard to go past a good roast chook or confit duck when the weather gets chilly. These are even better when they're paired with some root vegetables pulled from the veggie patch and roasted in duck fat.

My love of baking comes out in full force (I had a side business baking tarts while I was a young apprentice). Anzac bikkies often get a look-in, or I might make a classic self-saucing pudding to round off a meal.

Generosity lies at the heart of this food, along with a lack of fuss. Although there's nothing fancy here, there's a sense of indulgence that only a leisurely pace can bring. It's the kind of cooking that feeds the soul and I reckon just about all Aussies can relate to this warming country fare.

BANANA and RICOTTA FRENCH TOAST

/

The smell of French toast cooking in our house means it's the weekend.
On weekdays, it's all about getting everyone out the door as smoothly
as possible, but weekends mean we can take our time a little more and
enjoy this treat of a breakfast.

3 eggs
100 ml (3½ fl oz) milk
300 g (10½ oz) firm ricotta
1 tablespoon icing (confectioners')
    sugar, sieved
1 tablespoon brown sugar
Scraped seeds of ½ vanilla bean or
    ½ teaspoon vanilla extract
Finely grated zest of 1 orange
Pinch of ground cinnamon, plus extra
    to serve

8 thick slices of brioche or
    soft white bread
2 tablespoons vegetable oil
1 tablespoon butter
4 bananas, peeled and thickly sliced
Maple syrup, to serve

Preheat the oven to 180°C (350°F). Whisk the eggs and milk in a bowl to combine, then pour into a baking tray.

Mix the ricotta, sugars, vanilla, orange zest, cinnamon and a pinch of sea salt in a bowl to combine, then spread the mixture thickly over half the bread slices and sandwich with the remaining bread slices. Place the bread in the egg mixture and stand to soak for about 1–2 minutes, then carefully turn and soak the remaining side.

Heat the oil and butter in a large frying pan over a medium heat until the butter is foaming. Add the sandwich stacks to the pan,

making sure to drain off any excess egg mixture, and cook for about 1–2 minutes or until golden brown on the base. Carefully turn and cook on the remaining side for a further 1–2 minutes or until golden brown. Transfer to a baking tray lined with baking paper and bake for 3–4 minutes until warmed through.

Serve hot, topped with sliced banana, scattered with a little cinnamon and drizzled with maple syrup.

THICK APPLE HOTCAKES

As soon as the cooler weather rolls in, it's time to whip up a batch of these apple hotcakes – they're thick and fluffy, with a little tang and texture from the tart Granny Smith apples. A dollop of ricotta or natural yoghurt and a drizzle of honey makes them irresistible. Truth be told, they'd make an excellent dessert too – just add ice cream.

150 g (5$\frac{1}{2}$ oz/1 cup) plain
   (all-purpose) flour
150 g (5$\frac{1}{2}$ oz/1 cup) wholemeal flour
55 g (2 oz/$\frac{1}{4}$ cup) caster (superfine) sugar
1 teaspoon baking powder
$\frac{1}{2}$ teaspoon bicarbonate of soda
   (baking soda)
$\frac{3}{4}$ teaspoon mixed spice
350 g (12 oz/1$\frac{1}{3}$ cups) plain yoghurt

125 ml (4 fl oz/$\frac{1}{2}$ cup) milk
2 eggs
1$\frac{1}{2}$ tablespoons melted butter
Finely grated zest and juice of $\frac{1}{2}$ orange
1 teaspoon vanilla extract
3 Granny Smith apples
Vegetable oil, for frying
Ricotta, honey and coarsely chopped
   toasted hazelnuts, to serve

Preheat the oven to 150°C (300°F). Combine the flours, sugar, baking powder, bicarbonate of soda, mixed spice and a pinch of sea salt in a bowl and whisk to combine, then make a well in the centre. Whisk the yoghurt, milk, eggs, butter, orange zest and juice and vanilla in a bowl until smooth. Add to the well and gradually whisk until smooth and combined. Peel and coarsely grate the apples and fold into the pancake batter.

Heat a splash of the oil in a large non-stick frying pan over a medium heat. Add rough third-cupfuls of the batter to the pan,

leaving a little space between each for the batter to spread, and cook for 1–2 minutes until golden brown on the base and small bubbles appear on the surface. Turn and cook the other side, then transfer to a wire rack placed on a baking tray to keep warm in the oven while you cook the remaining hotcakes. Wipe out the pan with paper towel between batches.

To serve, pile the apple hotcakes on serving plates, top with a generous spoonful of ricotta, drizzle with honey and scatter with the chopped hazelnuts.

DATE SCONES

There's nothing that says rural Australia more than a scone – they make me think of small town shows and the Country Women's Association. Make sure to have a light touch when you're bringing your dough together – if you overwork it, the scones will be heavy and definitely not show-worthy! These date-filled beauties are as close as I can get to the ones my nan Valda used to make. Be sure to serve them warm.

350 g (12 oz/2$\frac{1}{3}$ cups) self-raising flour
2 tablespoons caster (superfine) sugar, plus extra for dusting
$\frac{1}{2}$ teaspoon mixed spice
3 tablespoons unsalted butter, chilled and cut into small dice
175 ml (5$\frac{1}{2}$ fl oz) milk

1 egg
Finely grated zest of 1 orange
180 g (6$\frac{1}{2}$ oz/1 cup) dried dates, pitted and cut into quarters
1 lightly beaten egg yolk, for brushing
Jam and clotted cream, to serve

Preheat the oven to 180°C (350°F) and line a baking tray with baking paper. Sieve the flour, sugar, mixed spice and a pinch of salt together into a bowl, add the butter and, using your fingertips, rub the butter into the flour. Make a well in the centre of the flour.

Mix the milk, egg and orange zest in a separate bowl to combine, then pour into the well. Add the dates and mix lightly to form a soft dough. Turn onto a lightly floured surface, roll to 5 cm (2 inches) thick, then cut out rounds with a 7 cm (3 inch) diameter pastry cutter. Re-roll the scraps once and repeat. Place the scones on the tray, brush the tops with the egg yolk and dust with sugar.

Bake for 10–12 minutes until golden brown and serve warm with jam and clotted cream.

BANANA BREAD with CINNAMON CRUMBLE TOPPING

It seemed to happen overnight, but suddenly every café had banana bread on its breakfast menu. When you think about it, it's really just cake for breakfast, but I won't tell anyone if you won't!

2 very ripe bananas (about 200 g/
    7oz), peeled and coarsely chopped
2 eggs
3 tablespoons vegetable oil
1 teaspoon vanilla extract
200 g (7 oz/$1\frac{1}{3}$ cups) plain
    (all-purpose) flour
100 g ($3\frac{1}{2}$ oz/scant $\frac{1}{2}$ cup) caster
    (superfine) sugar
100 g ($3\frac{1}{2}$ oz/$\frac{1}{2}$ cup) brown sugar
10 g ($\frac{1}{4}$ oz) baking powder

CINNAMON CRUMBLE TOPPING
40 g ($1\frac{1}{2}$ oz/scant $\frac{1}{4}$ cup) brown sugar
25 g (1 oz/scant $\frac{1}{4}$ cup) plain
    (all-purpose) flour
$\frac{1}{2}$ teaspoon ground cinnamon
1 tablespoon chilled butter, diced

Preheat the oven to 190°C (375°F) and grease and line an 11 x 21 cm (4 x 8 inch) loaf tin with baking paper, letting the paper overhang the sides by 5 cm (2 inches) or so. Process the banana, eggs, vegetable oil and vanilla in a food processor until very smooth.

Meanwhile, combine the dry ingredients and a good pinch of salt in a large bowl, whisk to combine, then make a well in the centre. Add the banana mixture to the well and gradually whisk until smooth and combined, then pour into the tin.

To make the cinnamon crumble topping, rub the ingredients and a pinch of salt in a bowl to combine and form clumps, then scatter over the batter and bake the bread for 1 hour 15 minutes– 1 hour 20 minutes until golden brown and risen and a skewer inserted into the centre withdraws clean. Cover the loaf with foil if it is browning too quickly.

Cool in the tin for 10 minutes, then use the excess paper to lift the loaf out of the tin and transfer to a wire rack. Serve warm or cool on the day of making, or serve toasted a few days later.

LEMON BUTTER with TOAST

Lemon curd is one of those old-school recipes that I never get sick of. I make
a big batch when lemons are at their juiciest and have it on hand to fill a
sweet pastry case for the quickest lemon tart, or to serve alongside scones
with clotted cream. But I probably like it best spread as thickly as possible
on toasted sourdough bread for brekky.

Finely grated zest and juice of 2 lemons
120 g (4$\frac{1}{4}$ oz) caster (superfine) sugar
5 eggs

160 g (5$\frac{1}{2}$ oz/$\frac{2}{3}$ cup) butter, diced
1 loaf of sourdough bread, thickly sliced

Combine the lemon zest and juice, sugar and eggs in a saucepan
and whisk until smooth, then place over a low heat and stir
continuously for 4–5 minutes with a wooden spoon until the
mixture thickens and coats the back of the spoon.

Add the butter, a few cubes at a time, stirring continuously until
all the butter is incorporated before adding more, then strain
through a sieve into a sterilised jar and refrigerate to chill for
about 3–4 hours.

To serve, lightly toast the sourdough bread and spread thickly
with the lemon butter. This recipe makes about 2 cups and will
keep, refrigerated, for up to 2 weeks.

EGG, BACON and TOMATO TART

This hearty tart is excellent for a leisurely breakfast or brunch. Get a step ahead and prepare the pastry case the day before, then all you have to do on the day is fill and bake it and wait for some seriously mouthwatering smells to fill the kitchen.

200 g (7 oz) sour cream or crème fraîche

2 teaspoons chopped thyme leaves, plus extra to serve

2 teaspoons Dijon mustard

150 g ($5\frac{1}{2}$ oz) cherry tomatoes, halved

2 vine-ripened tomatoes, cut into wedges

6 rindless smoky bacon rashers

6 eggs

2 tablespoons single (pure/ pouring) cream

2 tablespoons finely grated cheddar cheese

CHEDDAR PASTRY

125 g ($4\frac{1}{2}$ oz/scant 1 cup) plain (all-purpose) flour

125 g ($4\frac{1}{2}$ oz/scant 1 cup) wholemeal flour

150 g ($5\frac{1}{2}$ oz/scant $\frac{2}{3}$ cup) chilled butter, diced

100 g ($3\frac{1}{2}$ oz) cheddar cheese, coarsely grated

1 egg

1 tablespoon white vinegar

To make the cheddar pastry, combine the flours, butter, cheddar and a pinch of salt in a food processor and pulse until combined, but still with small lumps of butter in the mixture. Tip onto a work surface and make a well in the centre. Combine the egg and vinegar in a bowl, mixing with a fork, then add to the well, gently incorporating into the dry ingredients until a rough dough forms. Lightly knead to form into a disc, wrap in plastic wrap and refrigerate to rest for 1 hour.

Roll out the pastry on a lightly floured work surface to a rough 30 x 40 cm (12 x 16 inch) rectangle and line a 20 x 30 cm (8 x 12 inch) baking tray, pressing into the corners of the tray, then trim so the edges overhang the sides by about 2 cm ($\frac{3}{4}$ inch). Refrigerate until required.

Preheat the oven to 180°C (350°F). Stir the sour cream, thyme and mustard in a bowl to combine, spread in the base of the tart, then scatter the tomatoes over the top, leaving six gaps (these gaps are where the eggs will fit). Tear the bacon into rough pieces and tuck around the tomatoes, then carefully crack an egg into each gap, being careful not to break the yolks. Drizzle over the cream, scatter with the cheddar and season, then gently fold in the overhanging pastry to form a rough border.

Bake for about 30–35 minutes until the pastry is golden brown and the eggs are set. Serve the tart warm or at room temperature, scattered with extra thyme.

ZUCCHINI and FETA FRITTERS with YOGHURT DIPPING SAUCE

These fritters are a tasty snack for vegetarians and carnivores alike. They're extremely versatile too – I love them with poached eggs for a weekend brunch or paired with a herb and tomato salad for a more substantial meal.

3 zucchini (courgettes), cut into julienne
    or coarsely grated
1 small handful coarsely chopped flat-leaf
    (Italian) parsley leaves
1 small handful coarsely chopped dill
1 small handful coarsely chopped
    mint leaves
1 spring onion (scallion), thinly
    sliced diagonally
Finely grated zest of 1 lemon, plus
    lemon wedges to serve
100 g ($3\frac{1}{2}$ oz) feta cheese,
    coarsely crumbled

3 eggs, lightly beaten
135 g ($4\frac{3}{4}$ oz/scant 1 cup) plain
    (all-purpose) flour
$\frac{1}{4}$ teaspoon baking powder
Olive oil, for shallow-frying

YOGHURT DIPPING SAUCE
150 g ($5\frac{1}{2}$ oz/$\frac{1}{2}$ cup) Greek-style yoghurt
3 tablespoons extra-virgin olive oil
Finely grated zest and juice of $\frac{1}{2}$ lemon
1 small garlic clove, finely chopped

To make the yoghurt dipping sauce, stir all the ingredients in a bowl to combine, season to taste, then cover and refrigerate for the flavours to develop while you make the fritters.

To make the fritters, combine the zucchini, herbs, spring onion, lemon zest and feta in a bowl and season generously. Stir in the eggs, flour and baking powder and season with salt and pepper.

Heat about 3 cm ($1\frac{1}{4}$ inches) of olive oil in a deep-sided frying pan over a medium–high heat and check the temperature by adding a little spoonful of the fritter mixture. If the mixture bubbles and rises to the surface, the oil is ready. Carefully add rough tablespoonsful of the mixture in batches to the oil and fry, turning occasionally, for 2–3 minutes until golden brown (be careful as hot oil may spit). Remove with a slotted spoon and drain well on paper towels. Season to taste and serve hot with the yoghurt dipping sauce. Squeeze over lemon wedges to taste.

ROAST BEETROOT SALAD with LEMON, YOGHURT and CARAWAY

There are so many great varieties of beetroot (beets) around these days – you could use a mix of golden and red baby ones to make this salad even prettier. Another nice touch would be to shave some raw baby beetroot over the top (target beetroot would look amazing). If the leaves of the beetroot are tender and in good shape, you could scatter a handful over the top as well – it's all about celebrating the versatility of this underrated veg!

15 baby beetroot (beets) (about
   3 bunches), trimmed and scrubbed
6 beetroot (beets), trimmed
   and scrubbed
2 teaspoons olive oil
$1\frac{1}{2}$ teaspoons caraway seeds
$\frac{1}{2}$ small red onion, thinly sliced
Extra-virgin olive oil, for drizzling

Juice of $\frac{1}{2}$ lemon, for drizzling
Coarsely chopped dill, to serve

YOGHURT DRESSING
280 g (10 oz/1 cup) Greek-style yoghurt
60 ml (2 fl oz/$\frac{1}{4}$ cup) lemon juice
2 tablespoons extra-virgin olive oil
1 garlic clove, crushed

Preheat the oven to 200°C (400°F). Place the baby beetroot and four of the beetroot in separate roasting tins with 60 ml (2 fl oz/$\frac{1}{4}$ cup) water in each, drizzle with olive oil, season, cover with foil and roast until tender – this will take 20–30 minutes for the baby beetroot and 50 minutes–1 hour for the large beetroot. When cool enough to handle, peel the baby beetroot and halve them, then peel the large beetroot and cut them into wedges.

Heat a small frying pan over a medium–high heat, add the caraway seeds and dry-roast for a minute or two until fragrant, then tip into a bowl and set aside.

To make the yoghurt dressing, whisk the ingredients in a bowl to combine and season to taste.

Peel the remaining beetroot and cut into julienne.

To serve, arrange the roasted beetroot on a platter with the onion and raw beetroot, drizzle with a little extra-virgin olive oil and lemon juice, to taste, and scatter with the chopped dill and toasted caraway seeds. Serve the yoghurt dressing alongside.

PULLED PORK SANDWICHES

Secondary cuts of meat have enjoyed a resurgence in popularity in recent years, and that can only be a good thing. The key is long, slow cooking to transform what could be a tough cut into something meltingly tender. This pulled pork would also be great served with barbecued corn or even the killer potato salad on page 164.

3 kg (6 lb 12 oz) pork butt (Boston butt or pork shoulder on the bone), skin off
12 soft burger buns

DRY RUB

3 tablespoons smoked paprika
3 tablespoons sea salt
1 tablespoon onion powder
1 tablespoon garlic powder
1 tablespoon English mustard powder
1 tablespoon brown sugar

BARBECUE SAUCE

200 ml (7 fl oz) apple cider vinegar
175 ml ($5\frac{1}{2}$ fl oz) tomato sauce (ketchup)
100 g ($3\frac{1}{2}$ oz) American yellow mustard
50 g ($1\frac{3}{4}$ oz/$\frac{1}{4}$ cup) brown sugar
1 garlic clove, crushed
$\frac{1}{2}$ teaspooon cayenne pepper

FENNEL SLAW

2 large fennel bulbs
1 tart green apple
1 small red onion
1 handful torn mint leaves
100 ml ($3\frac{1}{2}$ fl oz) olive oil
Juice of 1 lemon

To make the dry rub, mix all the ingredients in a bowl to combine well, then massage into the pork. Cover with plastic wrap and refrigerate to marinate for at least 2 hours and up to 24 hours.

Preheat the oven to 150°C (300°F). Place the marinated pork butt on a lightly oiled wire rack placed over a roasting tin, cover with foil and bake for 6–8 hours until the pork is falling apart, then rest for at least an hour.

Meanwhile, to make the barbecue sauce, combine the ingredients in a saucepan, season and bring to a simmer over a medium-

high heat. Reduce the heat to medium and simmer gently for 8–10 minutes until slightly thickened, then set aside

For the fennel slaw, shred the fennel, apple and onion as finely as possible on a mandolin, combine in a bowl with the mint, olive oil and lemon juice, season to taste and toss to combine.

To serve, coarsely shred the pork with two forks, then toss with enough barbecue sauce to coat well – pour in some of the pan juices too. Spoon a generous amount of pork and sauce onto the burger buns, top with the fennel slaw and serve.

PUMPKIN SOUP with PARMESAN CRISPS

Pumpkin soup is a no-fail crowd pleaser. I've given it a bit of a modern twist with parmesan crisps, which are puffed up by finishing in the microwave. If you don't have a microwave, cook the chips in the oven for a little longer until they are golden brown and break into shards. If you're feeling a little retro, serve the soup in scooped out baby pumpkins (squashes).

100 ml (3½ fl oz) olive oil
8 French shallots, thinly sliced
5 garlic cloves, thinly sliced
1 rosemary sprig
1 butternut pumpkin (squash), peeled,
    seeds removed, roughly diced

1.5 litres (52 fl oz/6 cups) vegetable stock
200 g (7 oz) parmesan cheese,
    finely grated
Finely chopped chives, to serve

Heat the olive oil in a large saucepan over a medium–high heat, add the shallots, garlic and rosemary and sauté for 3–4 minutes until tender and translucent. Add the pumpkin and cook, stirring occasionally, for 7–8 minutes until the pumpkin begins to break down a little. Pour in the stock, season, bring to the boil then reduce the heat to low–medium and simmer for 10–15 minutes until the pumpkin is tender.

Remove the sprig of rosemary, then blend with a hand-held blender until very smooth. Bring the soup back to a simmer, whisk in half the grated parmesan and season to taste.

While the soup is cooking, make the parmesan crisps. Preheat the oven to 180°C (350°F) and line a baking tray with baking paper. Sprinkle the remaining parmesan evenly over the paper and bake for 2 minutes until the cheese is only just melted. Cool on a chopping board for 1 minute, then cut into strips approximately 4 cm (1½ inches) wide. Place the parmesan strips on a microwave-proof plate and cook on full power in the microwave for 90 seconds until they puff up and become crisp.

To serve, ladle the soup into warmed serving bowls, scatter with chives and serve with the parmesan crisps.

PORK and SAGE SAUSAGE ROLLS

You'd be hard-pressed to find an Australian who doesn't feel nostalgic about the humble sausage roll – that stalwart of school canteens and kids' parties. There's a lot to love, especially when they're cooked with a home-made rough puff pastry, as they are here. You can play around with fillings and flavours – lamb and harissa or beef and rosemary – but pork and sage are my favourite.

1 tablespoon olive oil

1 onion, finely chopped

2 garlic cloves, crushed

3 teaspoons fennel seeds, crushed

40 g ($1\frac{1}{2}$ oz/$\frac{2}{3}$ cup) coarse
    sourdough breadcrumbs

80 ml ($2\frac{1}{2}$ fl oz/$\frac{1}{3}$ cup) milk

500 g (1 lb 2 oz) pork mince

1 tablespoon Dijon mustard

$1\frac{1}{2}$ tablespoons finely chopped
    sage leaves

2 teaspoons finely chopped
    rosemary leaves

2 egg yolks, lightly beaten with
    1 tablespoon water, for brushing

Sea salt, to sprinkle

Tomato relish, to serve

ROUGH PUFF PASTRY

200 g (7 oz/$\frac{3}{4}$ cup) chilled unsalted
    butter, diced

200 g (7 oz/$1\frac{1}{3}$ cups) plain (all-purpose)
    flour, plus extra to dust

1 tablespoon white vinegar

To make the rough puff pastry, beat 150 g ($5\frac{1}{2}$ oz/$\frac{2}{3}$ cup butter) and 60 g ($2\frac{1}{4}$ oz/scant $\frac{1}{2}$ cup) flour in an electric mixer until smooth, then spread on a piece of baking paper to a rough 15 x 25 cm (6 x 10 inch) rectangle. Place another piece of baking paper on top and roll lightly to smooth the surface, then refrigerate for an hour until chilled. Combine the remaining butter and a pinch of salt in a clean bowl and rub the butter into the remaining flour with your fingertips until fine crumbs form. Add the vinegar and 60 ml (2 fl oz/$\frac{1}{4}$ cup) iced water and mix to form a soft dough, then knead on a lightly floured surface until just smooth. Wrap in plastic wrap, refrigerate for an hour, then roll out on a floured surface to the same size as the butter mixture.

Place the butter rectangle on top of the pastry and turn the pastry stack so a short side is facing you. Fold the top a third of the way down, then fold up the bottom third to enclose. Wrap in plastic wrap and chill for 30 minutes. Place the pastry on a lightly floured bench with the layered seams facing you. Repeat the rolling, folding and chilling once more.

Meanwhile, to make the filling heat the olive oil in a saucepan over a medium heat. Add the onion and garlic and sauté for about 3–4 minutes until the onion is translucent. Add $2\frac{1}{2}$ teaspoons fennel seeds and cook for a minute or so or until fragrant, then set aside to cool. Combine the crumbs and milk in a bowl and stand for 10 minutes until the milk is absorbed. Add the pork, mustard, herbs and onion mixture, season generously and mix well. Cover and chill.

Preheat the oven to 200°C (400°F) and line a large baking tray with baking paper. Roll the pastry on a lightly floured bench into a 28 x 40 cm (11 x 16 inch) rectangle, then halve lengthways. Divide the filling lengthways down the centre of each piece of pastry and brush the edges with the yolk mixture. Roll to enclose, overlapping the seam slightly, halve each roll crossways and place seam-side down on the tray. Score the tops, brush with the yolk mixture and sprinkle with sea salt and the remaining fennel. Bake for 30–35 minutes until the pastry is golden brown and the filling is cooked. Slice the sausage rolls and serve hot with relish.

LENTIL SALAD with CELERIAC and APPLE

Lentils are great to give a bit of grunt to a salad – I love the small French-style green lentils as they hold their shape and don't turn to mush. This salad can be added to easily. Try shredded poached chicken or crisp pancetta or simply serve alongside roast pork or chicken for a perfect autumnal side dish.

220 g (7¾ oz/1 cup) French-style green lentils
1 fresh bay leaf
1 thyme sprig
50 g (1¾ oz/½ cup) walnuts
1 celeriac
1 red apple, unpeeled, cut into matchsticks and tossed with a squeeze of lemon
1 French shallot, thinly sliced

1 large handful torn flat-leaf (Italian) parsley leaves

WHOLEGRAIN MUSTARD DRESSING
2 tablespoons olive oil
2 tablespoons walnut oil
1½ tablespoons red wine vinegar
1 tablespoon wholegrain mustard
1 small garlic clove, finely chopped

Combine the lentils, bay leaf and thyme sprig in a large saucepan, cover with cold unsalted water by 4–5 cm (1½–2 inches) and bring to the boil over a high heat. Reduce the heat to medium–high and cook for 10–12 minutes until just tender. Drain, then discard the herbs, and transfer to a bowl to cool to room temperature.

Preheat the oven to 180°C (350°F). Spread the walnuts on a baking tray and roast for 4–5 minutes until golden brown. Cool, then coarsely chop.

To make the mustard dressing, whisk the ingredients in a bowl to combine, thinning to drizzling consistency with a little hot water if necessary, and season to taste.

Trim the tops off the celeriac, peel, cut into matchsticks and add to the lentils along with the apple, shallot, parsley leaves and walnuts. Drizzle over the mustard dressing to taste, toss to combine and serve.

SILVERBEET, LEEK and GRUYERE TART

/

Silverbeet is often overlooked, especially these days when kale is the new(ish) leafy green vegetable on the block. I love silverbeet paired with loads of butter, leek and garlic, which form the basis of the tart filling here. This is one of my favourite dishes for a leisurely lunch at the farm and if there are leftovers, they're just as good for breakfast.

225 g (8 oz/1½ cups) strong flour
1 teaspoon dried yeast
1 teaspoon caster (superfine) sugar
1 teaspoon fine salt
3 eggs, at room temperature
90 g (3¼ oz/⅓ cup) softened butter

SILVERBEET, LEEK AND GRUYERE FILLING
2 tablespoons butter, diced
1 leek, white and pale green parts only, thinly sliced

2 garlic cloves, finely chopped
400 g (14 oz/½ bunch) silverbeet (Swiss chard), half the stalks thinly sliced, leaves chopped into bite-sized pieces
100 ml (3½ fl oz) dry white wine
1 egg
1 egg yolk
150 g (5½ oz/⅔ cup) crème fraîche
100 g (3½ oz/1 cup) coarsely grated gruyère cheese
2 tablespoons thyme leaves

To make the tart crust, combine the flour, yeast, sugar and salt in an electric mixer fitted with a dough hook, add the eggs and knead for until combined. Gradually add the butter, a little at a time, kneading continuously for 4–5 minutes until glossy and the butter is completely incorporated. Transfer to a lightly oiled bowl, cover and stand in a warm place for about 2–2½ hours until doubled in size.

Meanwhile, for the silverbeet filling, melt the butter in a large saucepan over a low heat, add the leek, garlic and silverbeet stalks and sauté, stirring occasionally, for 4–5 minutes until tender. Add the wine, season and simmer for 2–3 minutes until the wine is almost completely evaporated. Stir in the silverbeet leaves and cook for 2–3 minutes until just wilted, then cool completely. Whisk the egg, egg yolk and crème fraîche in a bowl until smooth, stir in the silverbeet mixture, cheese and thyme and season.

Preheat the oven to 190°C (375°F). Knock down the dough, roll out on a lightly floured surface to a 35 cm (14 inch) diameter round and line a 25 cm (10 inch) pie tin or tart tin, letting the dough overhang the sides. Spread the silverbeet mixture around the base, fold in the edges, pleating as you go, then bake for about 40–45 minutes until golden brown and cooked through. Stand for 10 minutes, then serve hot.

KILLER POTATO SALAD

A great potato salad should be part of every cook's repertoire, but let's be honest – not all potato salads are created equal. I prefer a tangy vinaigrette-style dressing laced with plenty of mustard, rather then a heavy mayo dressing. Plenty of herbs add a burst of freshness and I love to add crisp bacon or speck and soft-boiled egg too. Dress the potatoes while they're still warm so they soak up as much of the flavour as possible.

600 g (1 lb 5 oz) scrubbed Kipfler or other salad potatoes, larger ones thickly sliced, smaller ones halved
2 small French shallots, thinly sliced
4 eggs, at room temperature
110 ml ($3\frac{1}{2}$ fl oz) olive oil
6 rindless streaky bacon rashers or slices of speck

1 garlic clove, finely grated
1 tablespoon lemon juice, or to taste
1 tablespoon red wine vinegar
1 teaspoon Dijon mustard
1 handful coarsely chopped flat-leaf (Italian) parsley
1 small handful coarsely chopped dill
1 small handful chives, finely chopped

Combine the potatoes in a saucepan with plenty of cold salted water to cover generously. Bring to the boil over a medium–high heat and cook for 15–20 minutes until the potatoes feel tender when you pierce them with the tip of a sharp knife. Drain and return to the saucepan to steam, adding the sliced shallots so the heat from the potatoes softens them slightly.

Meanwhile, cook the eggs in a separate saucepan of boiling water for 7 minutes (this is for soft yolks – if you prefer your eggs firmer, cook for another minute or two). Drain, refresh under cold running water and peel.

While the potatoes are cooking, make the dressing. Heat 1 tablespoon of the olive oil in a large frying pan over a medium–high heat. Cut the bacon or speck into 5 cm (2 inch) lengths, add to the pan and fry, turning occasionally, for 2–3 minutes until crisp, then transfer to a tray, keeping the fat in the pan. Return the pan to the heat, add the garlic and remaining oil and stir for about 30 seconds until the garlic is fragrant. Remove from the heat, add the lemon juice, vinegar and mustard, season to taste and whisk to combine. Taste to check the acidity – you might want to add a squeeze more lemon, remembering the acidity will mellow once you've dressed the potatoes. When you're happy with the balance, add the dressing to the potatoes, toss to combine and set aside to cool to room temperature.

To serve, add the bacon and eggs to the potato mixture along with the herbs, toss to combine and serve at room temperature.

CHICKEN COOKED UNDER A BRICK

I love cooking chicken this way, as the weight of the bricks ensures as much of the chicken skin as possible is in direct contact with the pan or barbecue, meaning you get ultimate crispness. If you don't have house bricks you could weight the chicken with a cast-iron pan instead.

1 free-range or organic chicken
(about 1.6 kg/3 lb 8 oz)
80 ml (2½ fl oz/⅓ cup) olive oil
Juice of 2 lemons, plus extra wedges
to serve

1 tablespoon finely chopped thyme
leaves, plus extra to serve
3 garlic cloves, finely chopped

To begin, you'll need to butterfly the chicken. Place the chicken breast-side down on a chopping board. Cut down each side of the backbone with kitchen scissors or a large sharp knife (reserve the backbone to make stock if you like). Remove the rib cage and wishbone, then turn the chicken over, open out flat and press down firmly with the heel of your hand to flatten the chicken out.

Combine the olive oil, lemon juice, thyme leaves and garlic in a container large enough to hold the butterflied chicken snugly in a flat layer, season generously, then place the chicken in the marinade. Turn to coat well, cover and refrigerate for at least 2 hours (or as long as overnight), turning the chicken occasionally in the marinade. Stand at room temperature for 30 minutes before cooking.

Heat a barbecue or a large, heavy cast-iron pan to a low-medium heat. Wrap two house bricks in foil and set aside. Drain the chicken from the marinade, place skin-side down on the barbecue or pan and weight with the bricks (if you're using a cast-iron pan instead of bricks, place a layer of foil over the chicken before you place the pan on top). Cook for about 15–20 minutes until a deep golden brown all over, remove the bricks, turn the chicken over, replace the bricks and cook for another 10–15 minutes until cooked through. Check by piercing the thighs with a skewer – the juices should run clear; if they have a pink tinge, return the chicken to the barbecue for 5–10 minutes and test again. Transfer the chicken to a tray, cover loosely with foil and rest for 10 minutes, then serve scattered with thyme and with lemon squeezed over the top.

MUSHROOM and BARLEY BROTH
with FRIED HERB SAUCE

/

There's a reason that mushrooms are described as meat for vegetarians – they're full of flavour and have a robust meaty texture. I've used a mix of big field mushrooms and smaller Swiss brown mushrooms, and if they're in season, I'll add a handful of wild mushrooms too. Dried porcini mushrooms add a rich umami element to this rustic broth.

20 g ($\frac{3}{4}$ oz) dried porcini mushrooms
1 tablespoon olive oil
1 tablespoon butter, diced
1 onion, diced
1 celery stalk, diced
1 carrot, diced
2 garlic cloves, finely chopped
150 g ($5\frac{1}{2}$ oz/$\frac{3}{4}$ cup) pearl barley
1 tablespoon plain (all-purpose) flour
1 litre (35 fl oz/4 cups) vegetable stock
250 g (9 oz) field mushrooms,
     thickly sliced

250 g (9 oz) Swiss brown (chestnut)
     mushrooms, halved
Finely grated zest of $\frac{1}{2}$ lemon

FRIED HERB SAUCE
125 ml (4 fl oz/$\frac{1}{2}$ cup) olive oil
2 tablespoons each sage, rosemary
     and thyme leaves
4 tablespoons finely chopped flat-leaf
     (Italian) parsley leaves
2 teaspoons lemon juice
2 teaspoons red wine vinegar
1 garlic clove, finely chopped

Place the dried porcini mushrooms in a large bowl, pour over 750 ml (26 fl oz/3 cups) boiling water and set aside to soak.

Heat the olive oil and butter in a large saucepan over a medium–high heat until the butter foams, add the onion, celery, carrot and garlic and sauté, stirring occasionally, for 5–6 minutes until the vegetables are tender. Add the barley and stir for a minute or two to toast and coat in the oil, then stir in the flour.

Add the stock, dried mushrooms and their soaking liquid (avoid any grit that may gather in the bottom of the bowl), bring to a simmer and cook for 20–25 minutes until the barley is almost tender. Add the mushrooms and simmer for 6–8 minutes until tender, stir in the lemon zest and season to taste.

While the soup is cooking, make the fried herb sauce. Heat the olive oil in a small saucepan over a medium–high heat until shimmering, add the sage and fry for 20 seconds until crisp. Remove the sage with a slotted spoon, then repeat with the rosemary and thyme. Set the oil aside to cool, then chop the fried herbs and combine in a bowl with the parsley, lemon juice, vinegar and garlic. Season, then stir in enough of the cooled oil to reach a drizzling consistency.

Serve the hot mushroom and barley soup drizzled with the fried herb sauce.

SMOKY BAKED BEANS with SOURDOUGH CRUMBS

Home-made baked beans are so different to the tinned variety – made from scratch with dried beans, they have excellent texture and, unlike tinned baked beans, aren't overly sweet. I add smoky bacon for a more complex flavour and top them with crunchy sourdough crumbs for extra texture. Serve with poached eggs and plenty of toast to mop up all those delicious juices.

350 g (12 oz/1¾ cups) dried borlotti beans, soaked overnight in cold water, drained
500 ml (17 fl oz/2 cups) chicken or beef stock
1 fresh bay leaf
1½ tablespoons olive oil
1 red onion, finely diced
2 garlic cloves, finely chopped
250 g (9 oz) rindless smoky bacon rashers or speck, cut into strips
1 teaspoon each smoked paprika and hot paprika
400 g (14 oz) tin of chopped tomatoes

2 tablespoons Dijon mustard
1½ tablespoons maple syrup
1½ tablespoons brown sugar
2 tablespoons apple cider vinegar, or to taste

CRUNCHY SOURDOUGH CRUMBS
70 ml (2¼ fl oz) olive oil
1 garlic clove, finely chopped
180 g (6½ oz/3 cups) coarse sourdough breadcrumbs
1 tablespoon each finely chopped sage and thyme leaves

Combine the beans, stock, bay leaf and 750 ml (26 fl oz/3 cups) cold water in a saucepan, bring to a simmer over a medium–high heat and cook for 10-12 minutes to parcook the beans. Drain, reserving the cooking liquid and discarding the bay leaf.

Meanwhile, preheat the oven to 140°C (275°F). Heat the olive oil in a large casserole dish over a medium–high heat, add the onion and garlic and sauté for 4–5 minutes until tender and translucent. Add the bacon and fry for 2–3 minutes until the fat begins to render, then stir in the paprika until fragrant. Add the tomatoes, mustard, maple syrup and sugar and season to taste with freshly ground black pepper (don't add salt at this stage or the beans won't cook), then add the beans and enough reserved cooking liquid to just cover (about 375 ml/13 fl oz/1½ cups). Cover with a tight-fitting lid and bake, stirring occasionally, for

1–1¼ hours until the beans are just tender. Remove the lid, stir in the vinegar and continue baking, uncovered, for 30–40 minutes until the beans are very tender, then season to taste.

Meanwhile, to make the crunchy sourdough crumbs, heat the olive oil in a frying pan over a medium–high heat, add the garlic and breadcrumbs and cook, stirring occasionally, for a minute or two, until evenly toasted. Remove from the heat, then add the herbs, season to taste and set aside.

Increase the oven temperature to 220°C (425°F). Divide the baked beans among individual ovenproof ramekins or bowls, scatter with the sourdough crumbs and bake for 10-15 minutes (place the bowls on an oven tray to catch any juices that may bubble over) until bubbling, crisp and golden, then serve hot.

CHICKEN NOODLE SOUP
with TARRAGON SAUCE

There's chicken noodle soup and then there's this chicken noodle soup. Simmering the whole chicken, skin and all, gives incredible depth of flavour, while a swirl of tarragon sauce to serve takes it all to a whole other level.

1 free-range or organic chicken
    (about 1.6 kg/3 lb 8 oz)
1 head of garlic, halved
2 thyme sprigs
1 fresh bay leaf
1 onion, diced
1 leek, diced
1 fennel bulb, diced, fronds reserved
    to serve
1 celery stalk, diced
1 floury potato, such as Sebago, diced
200 g (7 oz) dried egg noodles or pasta,
    such as fettuccine

TARRAGON SAUCE

30 g (1 oz) day-old crustless sourdough
    bread, coarsely torn
50 ml (1½ fl oz) lemon juice,
    plus extra for the broth
1 tablespoon tarragon or white
    wine vinegar
30 g (1 oz/¾ cup) tarragon leaves
10 g (¼ oz/¾ cup) flat-leaf (Italian)
    parsley leaves
1 garlic clove, finely chopped
150 ml (5 fl oz) olive oil

Place the chicken in a large saucepan or stockpot, add the head of garlic, thyme and bay leaf, pour over enough cold water to cover by about 5 cm (2 inches), then bring to a simmer over a medium–high heat. Reduce the heat to medium, half-cover with a lid and gently simmer for 1½–2 hours until the broth develops a rich flavour. If scum appears on the surface, scoop it off with a slotted spoon.

Add the vegetables to the pan and simmer for 25–30 minutes until tender, then remove the chicken from the pan, place on a plate and discard the garlic, thyme and bay leaf. When the chicken is cool enough to handle, coarsely shred the chicken (discard the skin and bones) and return to the pan. Check the seasoning and add a squeeze of lemon if you like.

Meanwhile, to make the tarragon sauce, soak the bread in the lemon juice and vinegar for 4–5 minutes until soft, then transfer to a food processor. Add the herbs and garlic and process until coarsely chopped, then add the olive oil in a steady stream and process to combine. Season and set aside.

Bring the broth back to a simmer, add the noodles and boil, stirring occasionally to stop the pasta sticking to the base of the pan, for 5–6 minutes until al dente. Serve hot, scattered with fennel fronds and a dollop of tarragon sauce.

POTATO GNOCCHI with SAGE and BURNT BUTTER

Feather-light gnocchi is the perfect heart-warming dish to serve when the weather turns cool and I often put it on the menu at Chiswick. It's easy to make at home and the kids can get involved in making it too – they'll have great fun helping to shape the dough. I've kept it simple and classic, serving the gnocchi with a burnt butter and sage sauce, but you could also add sautéed wild mushrooms to the pan if you like.

1 kg (2 lb 4 oz) even-sized Royal Blue, Desiree or Pontiac potatoes, unpeeled
150–200 g ($5\frac{1}{2}$–7 oz/1–$1\frac{1}{3}$ cups) plain (all-purpose) flour, plus extra
200 g (7 oz/$\frac{3}{4}$ cup) chilled butter, cut into cubes

1 handful sage leaves
1 garlic clove, finely chopped
Finely grated zest and juice of $\frac{1}{2}$ lemon
Finely grated parmesan cheese, to serve

Preheat the oven to 200°C (400°F). Place the potatoes on a rack in the oven and roast for 40–45 minutes until when you insert a skewer into the centre it meets with no resistance – the exact time will depend on your potatoes, so keep an eye out. Remove the potatoes from the oven, cut each potato in half and, working quickly, scoop out the centres into a bowl (use a tea towel to hold the potatoes so you don't burn yourself).

Push the potato through a ricer, or mash until smooth and press through a coarse sieve, then tip onto a work surface and make a flat mound. Sieve over three-quarters of the flour and season. Mix lightly with your hands to bring together and form a soft dough – be careful not to overwork. Pinch off a little dough and drop into a saucepan of simmering water – the mixture should hold together. If it doesn't, knead in a little more of the flour and test again, but be careful not to add too much or your gnocchi will be heavy.

Once the dough is of the right consistency, roll into 1.5 cm ($\frac{5}{8}$ inch) thick cylinders, then cut into 3 cm ($1\frac{1}{4}$ inch) lengths, pinching the centres of each. Cook the gnocchi in a large saucepan of simmering salted water for 1–2 minutes until the gnocchi rise to the surface.

While the gnocchi are cooking, melt 60 g ($2\frac{1}{4}$ oz/$\frac{1}{4}$ cup) butter in a large frying pan over a medium–high heat. Transfer the gnocchi from the water to the pan with a slotted spoon, shaking off excess water, and cook, tossing occasionally, for 1–2 minutes until lightly golden. Transfer to a platter, wipe out the pan and add the remaining butter. Cook for 3–4 minutes until nut brown and fragrant, add the sage, then stir in the garlic and cook until the sage is crisp. Remove from the heat and add the lemon zest and juice, spoon over the gnocchi, season to taste and serve hot with plenty of parmesan.

BARBECUE SIRLOIN with CHILLI and CORIANDER RELISH

Although the farm is lamb-focused, we also have Black Angus cattle, which I reckon produce some of the best beef around. We dry-age our beef at the farm for our own use, which produces great depth of flavour. Rather than cooking individual steaks, I like to cook one thick steak and slice it to serve.

$\frac{1}{2}$ teaspoon each ground coriander, ground cumin and smoked paprika

$\frac{1}{2}$ teaspoon sea salt

1 kg (2 lb 4 oz) dry-aged sirloin steak, about 4 cm (1$\frac{1}{2}$ inches) thick, at room temperature

1 tablespoon olive oil

CHILLI AND CORIANDER RELISH

1 handful coriander (cilantro) leaves

1 spring onion (scallion), thinly sliced

1 small garlic clove, finely chopped

150 ml (5 fl oz/$\frac{2}{3}$ cup) olive oil

2 small pickled chillies, thinly sliced

1 long green chilli, thinly sliced

Juice of $\frac{1}{2}$ lime, or to taste

Combine the spices in a bowl with the sea salt, then rub well all over the steak. Place on a tray, cover with plastic wrap and marinate at room temperature for 1 hour.

To make the chilli and coriander relish, pulse the coriander, spring onion, garlic and olive oil in a food processor to a coarse consistency, then stir through the chillies and lime juice and season to taste.

Preheat a barbecue or chargrill pan to a medium–high heat. Drizzle both sides of the steak with olive oil and barbecue or chargrill for 5–10 minutes until well browned, then turn and repeat – this will cook the beef medium-rare. Transfer to a baking tray and cover loosely with foil to rest for at least 10 minutes.

To serve, slice the steak across the grain and serve drizzled with the chilli and coriander relish.

BEER CAN CHICKEN

It may seem a bit undignified for the poor chicken, but cooking it this way results in a very juicy and flavoursome bird. You can either cook it in the oven (make sure you remove all but one rack and set that at the lowest possible position), or in a kettle barbecue (make sure there's enough height to fit the upright chicken). Use whatever beer takes your fancy – if it's a beer you like to drink, then you'll more than likely enjoy the flavour it imparts. I'd avoid anything too heavy though, as it will overwhelm the flavour of the chicken.

1 free-range or organic chicken
   (about 1.6 kg/3 lb 8 oz)
1 tablespoon vegetable oil
2 thyme sprigs, plus extra leaves to serve

375 ml (13 fl oz) can of beer (your choice)
Juice of $\frac{1}{2}$ lemon, plus extra wedges
   to serve

Preheat the oven or a kettle barbecue to 200°C (400°F).

Rub the chicken all over with the vegetable oil and season well. Pick the leaves from the thyme and sprinkle over the chicken.

Open the can of beer and pour out half (or take a couple of swigs if you prefer!). Place the beer in a roasting tin and place the chicken on top of the can, pushing it partway into the cavity so that the chicken sits upright over the can, Roast for 1 hour, checking that

the chicken and can are still upright, then remove from the oven and transfer to a tray to rest for 10 minutes.

Place the roasting tin with the pan juices over a high heat, add 100 ml (3$\frac{1}{2}$ fl oz) water and bring to the boil, scraping off any sediment that may have formed on the base of the tray. Simmer for a few minutes, squeeze in a couple of drops of lemon juice and season to taste, then serve scattered with extra thyme and with lemon wedges to squeeze over.

DUCK CONFIT with BRAISED RED CABBAGE

Making duck confit at home is a perfect rainy-day task – well, make that a two-day task, as you need to cure the duck overnight before you cook it. The result is well worth the effort. The melt-in-the-mouth texture and rich flavour is pretty hard to beat. Once the duck has cooked, you can use it straight away or it will keep for up to a month. I recommend making a double batch so you're a step ahead for the next time the confit craving hits, and I guarantee you it will.

200 g (7 oz/1½ cups) sea salt
6 garlic cloves, finely chopped
1 tablespoon finely chopped thyme leaves
2 fresh bay leaves, coarsely crushed
6 duck marylands
1.5 kg (3 lb 5 oz) duck fat, melted
    (see note)

BRAISED RED CABBAGE
1 tablespoon olive oil
1 red onion, thinly sliced

3 rindless smoky bacon rashers,
    coarsely chopped
2 garlic cloves, finely chopped
1 red cabbage, cored, outer leaves
    discarded, cut into rough 2 cm
    (¾ inch) chunks
120 ml (4 fl oz/½ cup) red wine vinegar
1½ tablespoons brown sugar
3 thyme sprigs, plus extra leaves to serve
1 fresh bay leaf
1 handful of coarsely chopped flat-leaf
    (Italian) parsley

To cure the duck, combine the salt, garlic, thyme and bay leaves in a bowl, then rub all over the duck, cover and refrigerate overnight to cure.

Preheat the oven to 120°C (235°F). Rinse the curing mixture off the duck legs, pat dry with paper towels and place in a single layer in a roasting tin. Cover with the duck fat and bake for about 2–2½ hours until the meat is almost falling from the bone. If you want to store the duck at this stage, scatter a little salt in the base of an ovenproof ceramic dish large enough to hold the duck legs snugly in a single layer and add the duck. Strain the duck fat over the duck legs to cover completely by at least 2 cm (¾ inch). Cover and refrigerate until required – at this stage the duck will keep for up to a month (when ready to cook, soften the duck fat first to make it easier to remove the legs, which I find easiest to do in a low oven). Alternatively, remove the duck and set aside on a tray.

To make the braised red cabbage, heat the olive oil (or a heaped tablespoon of duck fat from the confit) in a large saucepan over

a medium–high heat, add the onion, bacon and garlic and fry for a few minutes until the onion is tender. Add the cabbage to the pan and stir for 4–5 minutes until the cabbage begins to wilt, then add the vinegar, sugar, thyme and bay leaf, season, cover with a lid and simmer, stirring occasionally, for 40–45 minutes until tender. Discard the thyme and bay leaf, check the seasoning and stir through the parsley.

Preheat the oven to 180°C (350°F). Heat a large frying pan over a medium–high heat, add the duck confit, skin-side down, and fry for 4–5 minutes until the skin is crisp and golden brown – you won't need to add any fat to the pan as the confit has enough fat of its own. Finish in the oven for another 2–3 minutes to heat through. Serve with the braised red cabbage.

NOTE You can buy duck fat in tins or jars from delicatessens and specialty food shops. It can be expensive to buy, but it can be reused several times, and I like to have some handy to use for roasting vegetables.

WHOLE ROAST CAULIFLOWER with ANCHOVY and GARLIC BUTTER

Roasting makes pretty much any vegetable tastier – especially cauliflower. I like to roast the cauliflower whole and douse it in an anchovy and garlic butter to serve. It makes a great accompaniment to roast pork or chicken, but could also be a meal in its own right, served with a crisp green salad and crusty bread to mop up all those buttery juices.

1 cauliflower, large stalk trimmed
Olive oil, for drizzling
150 ml (5 fl oz/$\frac{2}{3}$ cup) dry white wine
100 g ($3\frac{1}{2}$ oz/$\frac{1}{3}$ cup) butter, diced
2 teaspoons chopped thyme leaves

4 anchovies, finely chopped
1 garlic clove, finely chopped
Finely grated zest of 1 lemon, plus
    wedges to serve
$\frac{1}{2}$ teaspoon chilli flakes

Preheat the oven to 190°C (375°F). Place the cauliflower in a roasting tin large enough to hold it snugly, drizzle generously with the olive oil and rub in all over to coat well. Season and add the wine to the tin, then roast, drizzling occasionally with a little extra oil, for 1–1$\frac{1}{2}$ hours until golden brown and the cauliflower is very tender when the centre is pierced with a sharp knife.

Melt the butter in a saucepan over a medium–high heat and cook for 5–6 minutes until nut brown. Remove from the heat and stir in the thyme, anchovies, garlic, lemon zest and chilli, season to taste and spoon over the cauliflower. Serve hot, scattered with extra thyme and with the lemon wedges.

ROASTED HEIRLOOM CARROTS with CUMIN and GOAT'S CURD

At Chiswick Woollahra we often make a feature of the beautiful vegetables that come from our kitchen garden. When baby carrots are at their peak, it makes sense to give them pride of place, as I have in this recipe – all you need are one or two ingredients to enhance their flavour. If you can get a mix of different-coloured baby carrots, be sure to use them.

800 g (1 lb 12 oz) heirloom carrots (4 bunches), such as yellow, red, purple, white, Dutch, golf ball, trimmed
2 tablespoons olive oil, plus extra to serve

2 teaspoons cumin seeds
Juice of $\frac{1}{2}$ lemon
100 g ($3\frac{1}{2}$ oz) goat's curd
Baby coriander (cilantro), to serve

Preheat the oven to 180°C (350°F).

Using a small paring knife, scrape out any dirt from the base of the carrot stalks, then scrub the carrots clean and rinse under cold water. Pat dry with paper towels, then halve lengthways if they're large, otherwise leave them whole if they're smaller.

Combine the carrots, olive oil and cumin seeds in a roasting tin, season and toss to coat the carrots well in the oil. Transfer to the oven and roast for 20-25 minutes until the carrots are nicely caramelised and tender, then squeeze over the lemon juice. Arrange on a plate with dollops of the goat's curd, scatter with baby coriander and serve drizzled with olive oil.

POT-ROASTED CHICKEN with RICE and LENTILS

The beauty of this dish is the succulence of the chicken. Because it's roasted in a sealed pot with the stock, the chicken remains incredibly juicy. As a bonus, the rice and lentils beneath the chicken get to soak up all the chicken-y juices, layering up the flavour with lip-smacking goodness. Roasted baby carrots would be an excellent side dish.

1 free-range or organic chicken
    (about 1.8 kg/4 lb)
Finely grated zest of 1 lemon,
    reserve lemon for stuffing,
    plus extra wedges to serve
1 head of garlic, halved, plus 1 garlic clove
    extra, finely chopped
1 cinnamon stick
4 thyme sprigs
2 tablespoons olive oil
20 g ($\frac{3}{4}$ oz/$1\frac{1}{2}$ tablespoons) butter, diced
1 onion, thinly sliced

1 teaspoon each coarsely crushed
    coriander seeds and cumin seeds
180 g ($6\frac{1}{2}$ oz/1 cup) long-grain rice,
    such as basmati
50 g ($1\frac{3}{4}$ oz/$\frac{1}{4}$ cup) small green lentils or
    brown lentils
200 ml (7 fl oz) dry white wine
500 ml (17 fl oz/2 cups) chicken stock
Greek-style yoghurt and coarsely
    chopped mint and flat-leaf (Italian)
    parsley leaves, to serve

Preheat the oven to 200°C (400°F). Pat the chicken dry really well, inside and out, with paper towels. Quarter the reserved lemon and stuff the chicken cavity with it, along with the garlic head, cinnamon and thyme, tuck the wings under and tie the legs together with kitchen string.

Heat half the olive oil in a large frying pan over a medium heat, carefully add the chicken and turn occasionally for 5–6 minutes until browned on all sides. Set aside.

Meanwhile, add the butter and remaining oil to a flameproof casserole dish large enough to fit the chicken and heat over a medium–high heat until the butter foams. Add the onion and chopped garlic, stir occasionally for 3–4 minutes until just tender, then add the lemon zest, coriander seeds and cumin seeds and stir until fragrant. Stir in the rice and lentils to coat in the oil, add the wine and simmer for 2–3 minutes until reduced by half. Add the stock, bring to the boil, then add the chicken to the pan, breast-side up. Cover with a tightly fitting lid and bake for about 35–40 minutes until the chicken is cooked through and the rice and lentils are tender. Remove from the oven and stand, still covered with the lid, for 10 minutes, then season to taste and serve with the yoghurt, mint, parsley and lemon wedges.

SHEPHERD'S PIE

Shepherd's pie is one of those great classic dishes that, although considered inherently British, has worked its way into the Australian consciousness thanks to our colonial heritage. With its full-flavoured filling and creamy mashed potato top, it's pretty hard to go past. You can either bake a single large pie or, to keep the fights over the mash topping to a minimum, make it in individual ramekins.

1 teaspoon fennel seeds
2 tablespoons olive oil
1 kg (2 lb 4 oz) minced lamb
2 onions, finely chopped
1 carrot, finely chopped
2 garlic cloves, finely chopped
2 teaspoons tomato paste
(concentrated purée)
1 fresh bay leaf
1 rosemary sprig, finely chopped

3 tablespoons dry white wine
1 litre (35 fl oz/4 cups) chicken stock
2 tablespoons Worcestershire sauce
4 large floury potatoes, such as Sebago,
peeled and cut into large chunks
125 ml (4 fl oz/$\frac{1}{2}$ cup) milk
40 g (1$\frac{1}{2}$ oz/ 3 tablespoons) unsalted
butter, diced
1 egg yolk
3 tablespoons cornflour (cornstarch)

Heat a small frying pan over a high heat, add the fennel seeds and dry-roast for a minute or two until fragrant, then grind in a mortar and pestle.

Heat the olive oil in a heavy-based saucepan over a medium–high heat, add the minced lamb, season and fry, breaking up any clumps with the back of a spoon, for 3–4 minutes until browned all over. Drain off any excess fat, add the onion, carrot and garlic, season and sauté for 3–4 minutes until the vegetables soften. Add the tomato paste and cook for a minute, then add the fennel seeds, bay leaf and rosemary, followed by the white wine. Simmer for 1–2 minutes until the wine evaporates, then add the stock and Worcestershire sauce, bring to the boil and simmer for 40–45 minutes until rich and flavourful.

While the lamb is cooking, combine the potatoes in a large saucepan with enough cold salted water to cover generously and bring to the boil. Reduce the heat to medium and simmer for about 20–25 minutes until a knife is inserted easily, then drain in a colander and leave to steam for a few minutes – this will allow all the excess moisture to steam off. Return to the pan, mash with a potato masher, add the milk and butter and mash until smooth. Beat in the egg yolk and season to taste.

Preheat the oven to 180°C (350°F). Mix the cornflour and 100 ml (3$\frac{1}{2}$ fl oz) cold water in a bowl to a thin slurry, add to the lamb and simmer, stirring occasionally, for 4–5 minutes to thicken. Pour into four 500 ml (17 fl oz/2 cup) capacity ramekins or a 2 litre (70 fl oz/8 cup) capacity baking dish, then spoon or pipe the mashed potato over the top to cover completely. Bake for 30–35 minutes until the potato is golden brown and crisp. Stand for 10 minutes and serve.

BEER-BRAISED BRISKET with COLESLAW

Braising a whole piece of brisket is an investment in terms of time, so it's something I usually reserve for a long weekend at the farm. I'll marinate the meat for a day or two, then get the braise in the oven in the morning so the brisket is just right when dinner time rolls around. The time invested pays off though, with a rich, deep flavour and ultra-tender texture.

$1\frac{1}{2}$ tablespoons Dijon mustard

2 teaspoons each ground cumin, ground chilli, smoked paprika and freshly ground black pepper

2 teaspoons brown sugar

2 teaspoons sea salt

3 garlic cloves, finely chopped

1.5 kg (3 lb 5 oz) piece of beef brisket

1 tablespoon olive oil

1 onion, thinly sliced

3 thyme sprigs

1 fresh bay leaf

300 ml ($10\frac{1}{2}$ fl oz) light-flavoured beer

300 ml ($10\frac{1}{2}$ fl oz) veal stock

300 g ($10\frac{1}{2}$ oz) tinned chopped tomatoes

Soft white rolls, buttered, to serve

COLESLAW

200 g (7 oz) white cabbage, shaved on a mandolin

1 carrot, shredded on a mandolin

2 teaspoons finely chopped chives

2 tablespoons extra-virgin olive oil

2 teaspoons cider vinegar

2 teaspoons lemon juice

Mix the mustard, spices, sugar, salt and garlic in a bowl to a paste, rub all over the brisket, wrap tightly in plastic wrap and refrigerate for 1–2 days for the flavours to develop, then bring to room temperature for 1 hour.

Preheat the oven to 140°C (275°F). Heat the olive oil in a large flameproof roasting tin over a medium–high heat and brown the brisket well all over. Remove from the heat, pour off the excess fat from the tin, then scatter the onion and herbs in the roasting tin and place the brisket on top. Meanwhile, bring the beer, stock and tomatoes to a simmer in a separate saucepan, pour over the brisket, cover with foil and braise for 6–7 hours until the meat is fork tender and pulls apart easily. Remove the brisket from the roasting tin, cover loosely with foil, then skim the fat off the surface of the tin juices, season and simmer for 4–5 minutes to thicken slightly.

To make the coleslaw, combine the cabbage, carrot, chives, olive oil, vinegar and lemon juice in a bowl, season to taste and toss to combine.

Slice the brisket across the grain and serve stuffed into the soft rolls with the coleslaw, spooning some of the pan juices over.

SLOW-ROASTED LAMB SHOULDER with ROAST SWEET POTATO and TZATZIKI

It's fair to say I have a bias towards lamb – as a lamb farmer it would be odd if I didn't. Slow-roasted lamb shoulder is often on the menu at Chiswick and it's a winner with customers. Part of the appeal of lamb for me is its versatility. It works with so many flavour profiles – think Middle Eastern spices or more Mediterranean herbs such as rosemary and thyme. I love to pair it with tangy yoghurt as in this tzatziki, as it cuts through the fattiness of the lamb so beautifully.

1 tablespoon oregano leaves,
   finely chopped
1 tablespoon thyme leaves,
   finely chopped
2 garlic cloves, finely chopped
Finely grated zest and juice of $\frac{1}{2}$ lemon
70 ml ($2\frac{1}{4}$ fl oz) olive oil
1 lamb shoulder, bone-in (about 2 kg/
   4 lb 8 oz), at room temperature
250 ml (9 fl oz/1 cup) chicken stock
125 ml (4 fl oz/$\frac{1}{2}$ cup) dry white wine
3 sweet potatoes, cut lengthways into
   1 cm ($\frac{1}{2}$ inch) chips
Lemon wedges, to serve

TZATZIKI
300 g ($10\frac{1}{2}$ oz/$1\frac{1}{4}$ cups) Greek-style
   yoghurt
1 Lebanese (short) cucumber, coarsely
   grated and drained in a sieve for
   5 minutes
2 tablespoons extra-virgin olive oil
1 tablespoon lemon juice
1 garlic clove, finely chopped

Preheat the oven to 150°C (300°F). Combine the oregano, thyme, garlic, lemon zest and juice and 2 tablespoons of the olive oil in a small bowl and mix well, then season.

Cut several long, shallow incisions at intervals in the lamb, rub over the herb mixture, massaging well into the incisions. Place in a roasting tin, pour in the stock and wine, cover with foil and roast for $3\frac{1}{2}$–4 hours until the lamb is fork tender. Set aside to rest while you make the roast sweet potato.

Increase the oven temperature to 200°C (400°F). Combine the sweet potato and remaining oil in a bowl, season and toss to coat evenly. Spread on a large baking tray and roast, stirring occasionally, for 20–25 minutes until crisp and golden brown.

To make the tzatziki, combine the ingredients in a bowl, season to taste and mix well. Serve the slow-roasted lamb with its pan juices, the roasted sweet potato, tzatziki and lemon wedges.

BEEF and ALE PIE

Meat pies can get a bit of bad press, but this pie is sure to win over the non-believers. It all comes down to using good-quality meat. I love brisket for its deep flavour and, when it's cooked correctly, its wonderful fall-apart, melt-in-the-mouth texture.

1.2 kg (2 lb 10 oz) beef brisket, diced
Seasoned plain (all-purpose) flour, for
   dusting, plus 50 g ($1\frac{3}{4}$ oz/$\frac{1}{3}$ cup) extra
100 ml ($3\frac{1}{2}$ fl oz) vegetable oil
10 baby onions, trimmed and halved
8 garlic cloves, finely chopped
4 celery stalks, diced into 2 cm
   ($\frac{3}{4}$ inch) cubes

2 carrots, diced into 2 cm ($\frac{3}{4}$ inch) cubes
400 ml (14 fl oz) pale ale
1 litre (35 fl oz/4 cups) veal or
   beef stock
1 sheet puff pastry
1 lightly beaten egg yolk, for brushing

Preheat the oven to 150°C (300°F). Dust the beef in the seasoned flour. Heat half of the vegetable oil in a large ovenproof frying pan over a high heat, add the beef and fry, turning the beef occasionally, for 4–5 minutes until browned all over. Transfer to a plate and set aside.

Pour the remaining oil into the pan, add the onions, garlic, celery and carrot and sauté for 3–4 minutes until beginning to soften. Return the beef to the pan, add the ale and bring to the boil, then add the stock. Bring to the boil again, skim off any fat that forms on the surface, then cover with a lid and place in the oven to braise for 1–$1\frac{1}{4}$ hours or until the beef is tender.

Return the pan to a simmer over a medium–high heat on the stove. Stir the extra flour in a bowl with 125 ml (4 fl oz/$\frac{1}{2}$ cup) cold water to a slurry, add to the beef mixture, then stir to combine and simmer for 4–5 minutes until slightly thickened. Season, then transfer to a 1.75 litre (60 fl oz/7 cup) capacity casserole or pie dish and set aside to cool to room temperature.

Increase the oven temperature to 200°C (400°F) and line a baking tray with baking paper. Cut the puff pastry to slightly larger than the top of the casserole dish and brush the edge with the egg yolk. Invert the pastry over the beef and press the edges to the pie dish to seal. Brush the pastry with egg yolk, pierce a hole in the centre, place on the prepared tray and bake in the oven for 25–30 minutes or until the pastry is puffed and golden brown. Serve hot.

VEAL OSSO BUCCO
with SOFT POLENTA

There are two kinds of osso bucco – one rich with tomatoes and red wine, the other a lighter version, which is my favourite. It's called osso bucco bianco and, as the name implies, is a white version made with anchovies, white wine and chicken stock. I love to serve it on soft polenta to soak up the beautiful braising juices. I prefer coarse polenta for the texture, but it does take longer to cook. You could use an instant polenta if you prefer – follow the packet directions for the amount of liquid needed.

2 tablespoons olive oil
4 large or 8 small pieces veal osso bucco
1 onion, diced
2 celery stalks, thinly sliced
3 garlic cloves, finely chopped
4–6 anchovies
200 ml (7 fl oz) dry white wine
500 ml (17 fl oz/2 cups) chicken stock
1 fresh bay leaf
1 rosemary sprig
1 thyme sprig

SOFT POLENTA
500 ml (17 fl oz/2 cups) chicken stock
200 ml (7 fl oz) milk
100 g ($3\frac{1}{2}$ oz/$\frac{1}{2}$ cup) coarse polenta
60 g ($2\frac{1}{4}$ oz) finely grated
    parmesan cheese
30 g (1 oz/2 tablespoons) butter, diced

ROUGH GREMOLATA
1 handful coarsely chopped flat-leaf
    (Italian) parsley leaves
Finely grated zest of 1 lemon
1 garlic clove, finely chopped

Preheat the oven to 160°C (315°F). Heat the olive oil in a large frying pan over a medium–high heat and season the osso bucco well. Brown the osso bucco in the pan, then transfer to a roasting tin in a single layer. Add the onion, celery and garlic to the same frying pan and sauté for 4–5 minutes until tender, then stir in the anchovies until dissolved.

Deglaze the pan with the wine, simmer to reduce by half, then add the stock and herbs and bring to the boil. Season, pour over the osso bucco, then cover with foil and braise in the oven for 4–5 hours until almost falling from the bone. Set aside for 10 minutes.

When the osso bucco is almost cooked, start making your soft polenta. Bring the stock and milk to the boil in a wide saucepan over a medium–high heat and season generously. Gradually whisk in the polenta, reduce the heat to very low and simmer, whisking occasionally to begin with and more frequently as the polenta thickens, for 25–30 minutes until thick and no longer grainy. Whisk in the parmesan and butter to combine, check the seasoning and keep warm.

Meanwhile, combine the ingredients for the gremolata in a bowl and season to taste.

Serve the osso bucco and braising liquid spooned over the soft polenta and scatter with a generous handful of gremolata.

ROAST CHICKEN with SAGE and ONION STUFFING

What's not to love about a classic roast chook? We have a version on the menu at Chiswick and it's something we can never take off, it's so popular. A good-quality chicken is key here. This makes for the perfect Sunday lunch or dinner, served with golden roast potatoes and crushed peas. Be warned, there'll be a tussle over the stuffing – it's very addictive!

1 free-range or organic chicken
    (about 1.6 kg/3 lb 8 oz),
    at room temperature
60 ml (2 fl oz/$\frac{1}{4}$ cup) vegetable oil
1 tablespoon plain (all-purpose) flour
500 ml (17 fl oz/2 cups) chicken stock

SAGE AND ONION STUFFING
75 g (2$\frac{1}{2}$ oz/$\frac{1}{3}$ cup) butter, diced
1 onion, finely chopped
2 garlic cloves, finely chopped

100 g (3$\frac{1}{2}$ oz/1$\frac{2}{3}$ cups) panko crumbs
$\frac{1}{2}$ bunch sage, leaves picked and coarsely
    chopped, plus extra leaves to serve
$\frac{1}{2}$ bunch flat-leaf (Italian) parsley,
    leaves picked and coarsely chopped,
    plus extra leaves to serve
3 rosemary sprigs, leaves picked
    and coarsely chopped, plus extra
    leaves to serve
1 Granny Smith apple, cored
1 lemon

To make the stuffing, melt the butter in a saucepan over a medium–high heat until the butter foams and becomes nut brown. Reduce the heat to medium, add the onion and garlic and fry, stirring occasionally, for 8–10 minutes until the onion is lightly caramelised. Stir in the panko crumbs and the herbs, then grate in the apple and the lemon zest. Season and set aside to cool.

Preheat the oven to 180°C (350°F). Loosely fill the cavity of the chicken with the stuffing, then tie the legs together using kitchen string and tuck the neck flap and wings underneath. Rub the chicken with a tablespoon of the vegetable oil, place in a roasting tin, season and squeeze over half the lemon. Roast, basting with the pan juices and drizzling with extra oil if necessary, for 50 minutes–1 hour until golden brown and cooked through. To test, insert a small knife or skewer between the drumstick and the thigh – if the juices run clear the chicken is cooked through; if they are tinged with pink, return the chook to the oven and test again in about 10 minutes. Transfer the chicken to a platter, cover loosely with foil and rest for 10 minutes.

To make the gravy, carefully tip the fat out of the roasting tin, being careful not to lose the juices that have formed. Place the tin over a medium–high heat, whisk in the flour, then cook for a minute or so. Gradually add the stock, whisking to combine, then simmer for 2–3 minutes until the gravy thickens. Tip in any juices that may have formed while the chicken rests, squeeze in the remaining lemon juice and season well, whisking to combine. Pass through a fine sieve and serve with the roast chook, scattered with extra herbs.

DUCK FAT-ROASTED ROOT VEGETABLES
with HORSERADISH CREAM

Roasting vegetables in duck fat gives them an amazing crispness and added flavour, and they just make sense served with a duck dish such as the duck confit with braised red cabbage on page 181. Duck fat roast potatoes are the classic rendition, but I love to add other root veggies to the mix too.

50 g (1¾ oz/¼ cup) duck fat
500 g (1 lb 2 oz) parsnips, peeled and halved lengthways
500 g (1 lb 2 oz) scrubbed small salad potatoes, such as Kipfler, halved lengthways
500 g (1 lb 2 oz) baby carrots, trimmed
350 g (12 oz) baby beetroot (beets), trimmed, scrubbed and halved
2 small red onions, cut into wedges
1 head of garlic, halved

1 small handful coarsely chopped flat-leaf (Italian) parsley leaves

HORSERADISH CREAM
300 g (10½ oz/1¼ cups) crème fraîche
2 tablespoons wholegrain mustard
1 tablespoon Dijon mustard
1 tablespoon finely grated horseradish
1 tablespoon lemon juice
1 garlic clove, finely chopped

Preheat the oven to 190°C (375°F). Spoon the duck fat into a large roasting tin and heat in the oven for a minute or two until the fat melts and heats up. Add the vegetables to the tin, season well, stir to coat in the melted fat, then roast, turning occasionally, for 1–1½ hours until the vegetables are beginning to brown and crisp and are tender when tested with a skewer.

Meanwhile, for the horseradish cream, combine the ingredients in a bowl and season to taste.

Serve the roasted vegetables scattered with the parsley and topped with the horseradish cream.

ROASTED LEG of LAMB
with a ROUGH MINT SAUCE

The Sunday roast – it has to be a lamb leg, doesn't it? I like to keep things simple and serve it with a rough mint sauce, which adds just the right amount of fragrant lift. The duck fat-roasted root vegetables on page 202 would be an excellent accompaniment.

2 garlic cloves, finely chopped
1 rosemary sprig, finely chopped
Finely grated zest of $\frac{1}{2}$ lemon and
    juice of 1
$2\frac{1}{2}$ tablespoons olive oil
1 lamb leg, bone in, shank on
    (about 2.5 kg/5 lb 8 oz)

ROUGH MINT SAUCE
75 g ($2\frac{1}{2}$ oz/$2\frac{1}{2}$ cups) coarsely
    chopped mint leaves
125 ml (4 fl oz/$\frac{1}{2}$ cup) olive oil
2 tablespoons white wine vinegar
Finely grated zest and juice of $\frac{1}{2}$ lemon
1 small garlic clove, finely chopped

Preheat the oven to 200°C (400°F). Stir the garlic, rosemary, lemon zest, half the juice and olive oil in a bowl and season. Place the lamb in a roasting tin, drizzle with the oil mixture and rub well all over. Season and roast the lamb, basting occasionally with pan juices, for 1 hour 20 minutes– 1 hour 25 minutes for pink, and another 15 minutes if you prefer well done. Cover the lamb with foil partway through cooking if it browns too quickly. Set aside to rest for 15 minutes, then squeeze over the remaining lemon.

To make the rough mint sauce, blend all the ingredients in a food processor or blender to a purée and season to taste. To serve, carve the lamb and serve with the pan juices and the rough mint sauce on the side.

BRAISED BEEF SHORT RIBS with POTATO-CELERIAC GRATIN

Beef and red wine are a perfect match, especially when the weather is chilly and we're talking about slow-cooking. Beef ribs are an excellent option for braising, especially when paired with a creamy celeriac and potato gratin.

2.2 kg (5 lb) beef short ribs,
    cut crossways into rough
    5 cm (2 inch) pieces
2½ tablespoons plain (all-purpose) flour
2½ tablespoons vegetable oil
2 carrots, coarsely chopped
2 celery stalks, coarsely chopped
2 onions, coarsely chopped
3 garlic cloves, finely chopped
1 tablespoon tomato paste
    (concentrated purée)
2 teaspoons Dijon mustard
500 ml (17 fl oz/2 cups) red wine
3 thyme sprigs, plus extra leaves, to serve
3 oregano sprigs, plus extra leaves,
    to serve
1 fresh bay leaf

1 litre (35 fl oz/4 cups) beef or veal stock
2 teaspoons red wine vinegar

POTATO-CELERIAC GRATIN
600 ml (21 fl oz) single (pure/pouring)
    cream
3 thyme sprigs
2 garlic cloves, finely chopped
Grating of fresh nutmeg
800 g (1 lb 12 oz) floury potatoes,
    peeled and thinly sliced
2 celeriac, peeled and thinly sliced
50 g (1¾ oz/½ cup) finely grated
    parmesan cheese
30 g (1 oz/2 tablespoons) butter, diced

Preheat the oven to 170°C (325°F). Dust the ribs in the flour and season (reserve any unused flour). Heat the vegetable oil in a casserole dish over a medium–high heat, add the ribs in batches and brown well for 7–8 minutes. Transfer to a plate and pour any excess fat from the dish, leaving a few tablespoons in the bottom.

Add the carrot, celery and onion and fry, stirring frequently, for 4–5 minutes until golden brown. Stir in the garlic until fragrant, then stir in the tomato paste, mustard and any remaining flour and cook for 2 minutes, stirring often, until the mixture darkens.

Return the ribs to the dish, add the wine and herbs and simmer for 15–20 minutes until the wine reduces by half. Add the stock, bring to the boil, season, cover and transfer to the oven to braise for 2–2½ hours until the meat is almost falling from the bone. Stir in the vinegar, then stand for 15 minutes and skim any fat from the surface of the sauce.

Meanwhile, for the potato-celeriac gratin, bring the cream, thyme, garlic and nutmeg to a simmer in a saucepan over a medium–high heat, remove from the heat and discard the thyme. Combine the potato, celeriac and half the cheese in a large bowl, pour over the cream mixture to just cover the vegetables (you may not need all the cream mixture), season generously, then mix well to combine.

Transfer to a 1.5 litre (52 fl oz/6 cup) capacity ovenproof dish, scatter with the remaining cheese and dot with the butter. Place in the oven for the last 1½ hours of the ribs' cooking. Then, when the beef is resting, increase the oven to 200°C (400°F) and cook for another 10–15 minutes until bubbling and golden brown. Stand for 10 minutes, then serve with the braised short ribs, scattered with extra herbs.

ROASTED PORK SHOULDER with CRUSHED CELERIAC and APPLE RELISH

Pork shoulder gets a bit overlooked, I think. It's not the prettiest cut of meat, but it is full of flavour. When it's slow-roasted, it manages to deliver on two fronts: crisp and crunchy crackling and succulent meat. What's not to love?

2 kg (4 lb 8 oz) boneless pork shoulder
1 tablespoon Dijon mustard
2 teaspoons honey
1 teaspoon fennel seeds, coarsely crushed
1 garlic clove, finely chopped
Finely grated zest and juice of $\frac{1}{2}$ orange
1 teaspoon sea salt flakes
$2\frac{1}{2}$ tablespoons olive oil
1 large celeriac, peeled and cut into rough 2 cm ($\frac{3}{4}$ inch) cubes

2 garlic cloves, finely chopped
3 thyme sprigs
200 ml (7 fl oz) chicken stock
2 tablespoons butter, diced

QUICK APPLE RELISH
3 Granny Smith apples, diced
100 ml ($3\frac{1}{2}$ fl oz) dry apple cider
2 tablespoons apple cider vinegar
1 tablespoon caster (superfine) sugar
1 thyme sprig

Preheat the oven to 200°C (400°F). Score the pork skin at 1 cm ($\frac{1}{2}$ inch) intervals with a very sharp knife, then turn the meat over and make several incisions in the flesh.

Combine the mustard, honey, fennel seeds, garlic, orange zest and juice in a bowl, season, then rub all over the pork flesh (don't rub it on the skin). Wrap the meat tightly in baking paper and foil, leaving the skin exposed, then rub the sea salt into the skin.

Place skin-side up in a roasting tin, roast for 15–20 minutes to begin to crisp the skin, then reduce the oven temperature to 160°C (315°F) and roast for 3–3$\frac{1}{2}$ hours until the pork is fall-apart tender – check inside the foil every now and again and add a little water if the parcel is dry. Set aside to rest for 30 minutes.

To make the quick apple relish, simmer the ingredients in a saucepan over a medium–high heat for 10–15 minutes until the apples are tender, season to taste and set aside.

While the pork is resting, heat the olive oil in a large frying pan over a medium–high heat, add the celeriac and fry, stirring occasionally, for 4–5 minutes until golden brown. Add the garlic and thyme, stir briefly until fragrant, then add the stock, cover and reduce the heat to low, and cook for 15–20 minutes until the celeriac is tender. Add the butter, then coarsely crush the celeriac with the back of a spoon and season to taste.

To serve, carve the pork and serve with the crushed celeriac and apple relish, with some pan juices spooned over.

RIBOLLITA

Ribollita has a consistency that sits somewhere between a soup and a stew. It's full of hearty winter vegetables and is given an extra layer of flavour by adding a parmesan heel to the simmering mixture (never throw the end of the parmesan away).

2 tablespoons olive oil
1 carrot, diced into 1 cm ($\frac{1}{2}$ inch) pieces
1 red onion, diced into 1 cm ($\frac{1}{2}$ inch) pieces
1 celery stalk, diced into 1 cm ($\frac{1}{2}$ inch) pieces
2 garlic cloves, finely chopped
250 g (9 oz) tinned plum tomatoes
2 litres (70 fl oz/8 cups) vegetable stock
100 g ($3\frac{1}{2}$ oz) podded fresh or cooked dried borlotti beans

1 parmesan cheese heel
150 g ($5\frac{1}{2}$ oz) cavolo nero ($1\frac{1}{2}$ bunches), tough stalks trimmed, leaves coarsely chopped
$\frac{1}{2}$ bunch flat-leaf (Italian) parsley, leaves picked
Toasted ciabatta, to serve
Extra-virgin olive oil, for drizzling

Heat the olive oil in a large saucepan over a medium heat, add the carrot, onion, celery and garlic, season and sauté, stirring often, for 15–20 minutes until the vegetables are very tender and translucent, but with no colour.

Stir in the tomatoes, cook for another 10 minutes until the tomatoes begin to break down, then add the stock, borlotti beans and parmesan heel and simmer for 4–5 minutes until the borlotti beans are almost tender.

Stir in the cavolo nero and half the parsley leaves and simmer for 10–15 minutes until the cavolo nero and beans are tender and the soup has a thick, stew-like consistency. Stir in the remaining parsley and season to taste.

Discard the parmesan heel and serve hot with the ciabatta and drizzled with the extra-virgin olive oil.

CHOCOLATE CREAM BISCUITS

This is my homage to that great Australian bikkie, the Tim Tam. Although there have been all sorts of new flavours added to the range over the years, for me it's all about the original version. Here's mine.

160 g (5½ oz) plain (all-purpose) flour
40 g (1½ oz/⅓ cup) icing (confectioners')
    sugar, sieved
40 g (1½ oz/⅓ cup) Dutch-process
    cocoa, sieved
80 g (2¾ oz/⅓ cup) unsalted butter, diced
1 egg

100 g (3½ oz/⅔ cup) each dark chocolate
    buttons and milk chocolate buttons

CHOCOLATE CREAM FILLING
100 ml (3½ fl oz) single (pure/pouring)
    cream
80 g (2¾ oz/½ cup) dark chocolate
    buttons

Preheat the oven to 160°C (315°F) and lightly grease a baking tray. To prepare the biscuit dough, sieve the flour, icing sugar and cocoa powder into a bowl and add a pinch of salt. Add the butter, then rub in with your fingertips until the mixture resembles fine crumbs. Mix in the egg to make a dough, form into a disc, wrap in plastic wrap and refrigerate for 1 hour to rest.

While the biscuit dough rests, make the chocolate cream filling. Bring the cream to the boil in a small saucepan over a medium–high heat, remove from the heat and add the chocolate. Stand for 5 minutes, then stir until the chocolate is smooth and combined. Refrigerate until beginning to firm, then transfer to a piping bag and set aside.

Roll out the biscuit dough on a lightly floured work surface into a 5 mm (¼ inch) thick 20 x 50 cm (8 x 20 inch) rectangle, then cut into 4 x 8 cm (1½ x 3 inch) rectangles (use a ruler to help keep them even). Place the rectangles onto the prepared tray, bake for 10–15 minutes until crisp, then cool completely on a wire rack.

To prepare the chocolate coating, melt all the chocolate buttons in a bowl over a saucepan of simmering water (make sure the base of the bowl doesn't touch the water), stirring occasionally until smooth.

To assemble, pipe the chocolate filling over half of the biscuits, then sandwich with the remaining biscuits. Dip each of the chocolate sandwiches into the melted chocolate, then place on a tray lined with baking paper until set. Serve with a nice hot cup of tea.

LIME DELICIOUS PUDDING

This magical pudding is one that takes me straight back to my childhood. I was always amazed at how such a simple mixture turned into the delicate tangy custard on the bottom and the fluffy sponge mixture on top. It would be a crime not to serve this with vanilla ice cream or crème fraîche.

60 g (2¼ oz/¼ cup) unsalted butter
250 g (9 oz/1 cup) caster
    (superfine) sugar
Finely grated zest of 1 lime and juice of 2,
    plus extra grated zest to serve

3 eggs, separated
350 ml (12 fl oz/1⅓ cups) milk
35 g (1¼ oz/¼ cup) self-raising flour
Icing (confectioners') sugar and vanilla
    ice cream or crème fraîche, to serve

Preheat the oven to 180°C (350°F) and lightly butter a 1.25 litre (44 fl oz/5 cup) capacity baking dish. Beat the butter, sugar and lime zest in an electric mixer for 3–4 minutes until light and fluffy. Beat in the yolks to combine, then stir in the milk, flour and lime juice.

Whisk the egg whites and a pinch of salt in a clean bowl for about 3–4 minutes to stiff peaks, fold into the lime batter and pour into the baking dish.

Place the baking dish in a large roasting tin, pour in enough boiling water to come halfway up the sides of the dish and bake for 35–40 minutes until golden brown and spongy on the top.

Dust with icing sugar and lime zest and serve hot with ice cream or crème fraîche.

HONEY and MACADAMIA TART

Macadamias are indigenous to Australia, one of the original bush foods.
They have a beautiful waxy texture and sweet flavour that works well with
this buttery honey-scented filling.

SWEET PASTRY
300 g (10½ oz/2 cups) plain
 (all-purpose) flour
90 g (3¼ oz/¾ cup) icing
 (confectioners') sugar
180 g (6½ oz/¾ cup) butter, diced
1 egg
1 egg yolk, lightly beaten, for brushing

175 g (6 oz) honey
50 g (1¾ oz) brown sugar
50 g (1¾ oz) melted butter
30 g (1 oz) plain (all-purpose) flour
2 eggs
Finely grated zest and juice of ½ orange
½ vanilla bean, split and seeds scraped
500 g (1 lb 2 oz/3¼ cups) macadamia
 nuts, coarsely chopped

To make the pastry, sieve the flour and icing sugar into a bowl and add a pinch of salt. Add the butter, then use your fingertips to rub the butter into the dry ingredients until fine crumbs form. Mix in the whole egg until a dough forms. Wrap the pastry in plastic wrap, then place into the refrigerator to rest for 2 hours.

Roll the pastry on a lightly floured work surface to 5 mm (¼ inch) thick and line a 4 cm (1½ inch) deep, 24 cm (10½ inch) diameter tart tin, allowing the pastry to overhang the sides. Refrigerate for an hour to rest. Preheat the oven to 160°C (315°F). Trim the excess pastry, then line with baking paper and fill with raw rice or baking weights. Blind-bake for 10–15 minutes until the edges of the pastry are golden. Remove the baking paper and weights, brush with egg yolk and bake for another 5 minutes until golden brown.

Reduce the oven temperature to 150°C (300°F). Whisk the honey, sugar, butter, flour, eggs, orange zest and juice and vanilla in a bowl to combine, then stir in the macadamia nuts and a pinch of salt. Pour into the pastry case and bake, turning occasionally, for 50 minutes–1 hour until evenly golden brown. Set aside to cool slightly and serve warm or at room temperature.

RICOTTA and LEMON DOUGHNUTS

Doughnuts come in many shapes and sizes, although what most often comes to mind are the ring-shaped variety. These ricotta-flecked little numbers are more in the style of an Italian doughnut, and they're so incredibly easy to make – no proving or rolling required. Use a good firm ricotta from the deli counter rather than the ricotta you get in tubs, as it will be too wet for this purpose.

Vegetable oil, for deep-frying
200 g (7 oz/scant 1 cup) firm ricotta cheese, plus 50 g ($1\frac{3}{4}$ oz/$\frac{1}{4}$ cup) extra
2 eggs
75 g ($2\frac{1}{2}$ oz/$\frac{1}{2}$ cup) plain (all-purpose) flour

2 tablespoons caster (superfine) sugar, plus 200 g (7 oz/scant 1 cup) extra for dusting
$1\frac{1}{2}$ teaspoons baking powder
$\frac{1}{2}$ teaspoon ground cinnamon
1 vanilla bean, split and seeds scraped
Finely grated zest of 1 lemon

Heat the vegetable oil in a deep-fat fryer or large saucepan to 180°C (350°F). Beat 200 g (7 oz/$\frac{3}{4}$ cup) ricotta and the eggs in a bowl until smooth, stir in the flour, 2 tablespoons sugar, baking powder, cinnamon, vanilla seeds and half the lemon zest and mix to just combine. Stir in the remaining ricotta, trying to keep little chunks of ricotta throughout the batter.

Combine the remaining sugar and remaining lemon zest in a bowl and set aside.

Carefully add heaped spoonfuls of the batter in batches to the oil (be careful as the hot oil will spit). The doughnuts will form in the bottom of the oil, but will puff up and rise to the surface as they cook.

Deep fry, turning occasionally, for 3–4 minutes until golden brown, then remove with a slotted spoon, drain briefly on paper towels and toss in the lemon sugar. Serve hot.

RHUBARB CRUMBLE CAKE

Tart rhubarb is so good in baking, especially when paired with brown sugar and fragrant spices – as it is in this cake. The crumble topping adds another layer of deliciousness here. In theory, this cake will keep for a few days in an airtight container, but it's highly unlikely it will have to.

400 g (14 oz) rhubarb, trimmed and cut
 into rough 3–4 cm ($1\frac{1}{2}$ inch) pieces
110 g ($3\frac{3}{4}$ oz/$\frac{1}{2}$ cup) brown sugar
110 g ($3\frac{3}{4}$ oz/$\frac{1}{2}$ cup) caster (superfine)
 sugar
160 g ($5\frac{1}{2}$ oz/$\frac{2}{3}$ cup) softened butter
1 vanilla bean, split and seeds scraped
 or 1 teaspoon vanilla extract
Finely grated zest and juice of 1 orange
2 eggs
220 g ($7\frac{3}{4}$ oz) plain (all-purpose) flour
80 g ($2\frac{3}{4}$ oz/$\frac{3}{4}$ cup) hazelnut meal
2 teaspoons ground cinnamon
2 teaspoons ground ginger

1 teaspoon baking powder
$\frac{3}{4}$ teaspoon bicarbonate of soda
 (baking soda)
160 ml ($5\frac{1}{4}$ fl oz) buttermilk,
 well-shaken

CRUMBLE TOPPING
50 g ($1\frac{3}{4}$ oz/$\frac{1}{3}$ cup) plain (all-purpose)
 flour
50 g ($1\frac{3}{4}$ oz) brown sugar
3 tablespoons butter, cut into little cubes
40 g ($1\frac{1}{2}$ oz/$\frac{1}{4}$ cup) toasted hazelnuts,
 coarsely chopped

Preheat the oven to 170°C (325°F). Butter and line a 15 x 30 cm (6 x 12 inch) rectangular cake tin or a 23 cm (9 inch) round cake tin with baking paper. Toss the rhubarb in a bowl with 1 tablespoon of each of the sugars and set aside.

To make the crumble topping, rub the flour, sugar, butter and a good pinch of sea salt in a bowl until little clumps form, then mix in the hazelnuts. Spread the mixture on a tray, pressing together a little to keep clusters of mixture together, then put in the freezer while you make the cake batter.

Beat the butter, remaining sugars, vanilla and orange zest in an electric mixer for 2–3 minutes until light and fluffy, then beat in the eggs, one at a time, scraping down the sides and base of the bowl and beating to combine before you add the next egg. Add the flour, hazelnut meal, spices, baking powder, bicarbonate of soda and orange juice and mix on a low speed. Beat to combine, gradually adding the buttermilk as you do, until just smooth, then spoon into the cake tin.

Smooth over the top and then scatter over half the crumble mixture. Pile on the rhubarb and drizzle over any juices that have formed in the bottom of the bowl. You may need to pile the rhubarb up a bit – don't worry if it looks higgledy-piggledy, it will settle as it bakes. Scatter over the rest of the crumble topping and bake for 50 minutes–1 hour until golden brown and firm in the centre. Cool slightly in the tin, then transfer to a wire rack to cool completely, or serve warm.

NAN'S FRUIT CAKE

The scent of the rich, dark spices filling the kitchen as this cake bakes reminds me of my nan, who'd cook this every year at Christmas. There's no reason you couldn't enjoy it at other times of the year too – to my mind it's even better in cold weather. I like to drizzle the cake with a little brandy while it's still warm for a hit of boozy flavour (it also helps the cake keep a little longer).

225 g (8 oz/$1\frac{1}{2}$ cups) plain (all-purpose) flour
$\frac{1}{2}$ teaspoon mixed spice
$\frac{1}{2}$ teaspoon ground cinnamon
$\frac{1}{4}$ teaspoon salt
200 g (7 oz/$\frac{3}{4}$ cup) unsalted butter, at room temperature
200 g (7 oz/1 cup) brown sugar
2 tablespoons treacle
1 tablespoon marmalade
$\frac{1}{4}$ teaspoon vanilla extract

4 eggs at room temperature, lightly beaten
200 g (7 oz/$1\frac{1}{3}$ cups) currants
200 g (7 oz/$1\frac{1}{4}$ cups) raisins
200 g (7 oz/ $1\frac{1}{4}$ cups) dried dates, coarsely chopped
200 g (7 oz/$2\frac{1}{4}$ cups) dried apple, coarsely chopped
100 g ($3\frac{1}{2}$ oz/$\frac{2}{3}$ cup) mixed candied citrus peel
100 g ($3\frac{1}{2}$ oz/$\frac{2}{3}$ cup) almonds, coarsely chopped

Preheat the oven to 150°C (300°F). Butter a 20 cm (8 inch) square cake tin and line the base and sides with baking paper. Sieve the flour, spices and salt into a bowl and set aside. Beat the butter and sugar in an electric mixer for 4–5 minutes until pale and creamy, add the treacle, marmalade and vanilla and beat until light and fluffy. Beat the eggs into the mixture little by little until well combined, then fold in the flour mixture followed by the dried fruit and almonds. Spoon the mixture into the tin, smooth the top and bake for about 3 hours until a skewer inserted into the centre of the cake comes out clean – if there's a little cake mix on the skewer, return the cake to the oven and cook for another 15–20 minutes. Cool in the tin for 20–30 minutes, then turn out onto a wire cake rack and cool completely. Store in an airtight container for up to 3 weeks.

MELTING MOMENTS

The name is a dead giveaway – these biscuits are so delicate they'll melt in your mouth. They're incredibly fragile when they're hot, so be sure to let them cool completely on the baking trays before you handle them. I'll warn you, this will be hard to do. They smell so delicious you'll just want to devour them straight away, but it's worth the wait!

250 g (9 oz/1 cup) unsalted butter,
    at room temperature
120 g ($4\frac{1}{4}$ oz/1 cup) icing (confectioners')
    sugar, sieved, plus extra for dusting
1 vanilla bean, split and seeds scraped
150 g ($5\frac{1}{2}$ oz/1 cup) self-raising flour
150 g ($5\frac{1}{2}$ oz/$1\frac{1}{4}$ cups) cornflour
    (cornstarch)

FILLING
100 g ($3\frac{1}{2}$ oz/$\frac{1}{3}$ cup) unsalted butter,
    at room temperature
120 g ($4\frac{1}{4}$ oz/1 cup) icing (confectioners')
    sugar, sieved
Finely grated zest and juice of 1 lemon

Preheat the oven to 150°C (300°F) and line a few baking trays with lightly greased baking paper. Beat the butter, icing sugar and vanilla seeds in a bowl for 4–5 minutes until very light and fluffy, sieve over the self-raising flour and cornflour, add a pinch of salt and stir to combine. Roll into walnut-sized balls and place on the tray, leaving 6–8 cm ($2\frac{1}{2}$–3 inch) spaces between each for the dough to spread.

Bake the biscuits, turning the tray partway through cooking, for 10–15 minutes until light golden brown, then cool completely on the trays.

To make the filling, beat the butter, icing sugar and lemon zest in a bowl until very pale, then add enough lemon juice to reach a thick spreadable consistency. Spread half the biscuits with icing, sandwich with the remaining biscuits and serve dusted with icing sugar.

ANZAC BISCUITS

It's pretty hard to go past an Anzac biscuit. Full of oats and the rich dark sweetness of golden syrup, there's a deeply held nostalgia for these classic biscuits. In my ideal world, I'd have a tin of these in the pantry at the farm at all times, but they seem to disappear as soon as they're made. They're perfect with a cuppa.

100 g (3½ oz/1 cup) rolled (porridge) oats
100 g (3½ oz/⅔ cup) plain
    (all-purpose) flour
70 g (2½ oz/⅓ cup) caster
    (superfine) sugar
50 g (1¾ oz/½ cup) desiccated
    (shredded) coconut

1 teaspoon bicarbonate of soda
    (baking soda)
1½ tablespoons warm water
125 g (4½ oz/½ cup) butter, melted
1 tablespoon golden syrup

Preheat the oven to 150°C (300°F) and line a few baking trays with baking paper. Combine the oats, flour, sugar, coconut and a pinch of salt in a bowl. Combine the bicarbonate of soda in a separate small bowl with the warm water, add to the dry mixture along with the melted butter and golden syrup and mix well to combine. Divide the mixture into 20 balls and place on the trays, pressing to flatten the biscuits slightly – leave 5 cm (2 inches) between each for the biscuits to spread. Bake for 15–20 minutes until dark golden brown, cool on the trays and store in an airtight container for up to 2 weeks.

INDEX

Published in 2017 by Murdoch Books, an imprint of Allen & Unwin

Murdoch Books Australia
83 Alexander Street
Crows Nest NSW 2065
Phone: +61 (0) 2 8425 0100
Fax: +61 (0) 2 9906 2218
murdochbooks.com.au
info@murdochbooks.com.au

Murdoch Books UK
Ormand House
26–27 Boswell Street
London WC1N 3JZ
Phone: +44 (0) 20 8785 5995
murdochbooks.co.uk
info@murdochbooks.co.uk

For Corporate Orders & Custom Publishing, contact our Business Development Team at
salesenquiries@mudochbooks.com.au

Publisher: Jane Morrow
Editorial Manager: Katie Bosher
Design Manager: Madeleine Kane
Project Editor: Kay Halsey
Design: Dan Peterson and Jacqui Porter, Northwood Green
Photographer: William Meppem
Stylist and Food Editor: Emma Knowles
Production Manager: Lou Playfair

A cataloguing-in-publication entry is available from the catalogue of the National Library of Australia at nla.gov.au.

ISBN 978 1 76063 123 9 Australia
ISBN 978 1 76063 405 6 UK

A catalogue record for this book is available from the British Library.

Colour reproduction by Splitting Image Colour Studio Pty Ltd, Clayton, Victoria
Printed by Hang Tai Printing Company Limited, China

IMPORTANT: Those who might be at risk from the effects of salmonella poisoning (the elderly, pregnant women, young children
and those suffering from immune deficiency diseases) should consult their doctor with any concerns about eating raw eggs.
OVEN GUIDE: You may find cooking times vary depending on the oven you are using. For fan-forced ovens, as a general rule,
set the oven temperature to 20°C (70°F) lower than indicated in the recipe.
MEASURES GUIDE: We have used 20 ml (4 teaspoon) tablespoon measures. If you are using a 15 ml (3 teaspoon) tablespoon
add an extra teaspoon of the ingredient for each tablespoon specified.